why architecture matters

yale

university

press

new haven

and

london

paul

goldberger

why

architecture

matters

Published with assistance from the Louis Stern Memorial Fund.
Designed by Nancy Ovedovitz and set in Adobe Garamond
type by Keystone Typesetting, Inc., Orwigsburg,
Pennsylvania. Printed in the United States of America.
Photo editor: Natalie Matutschovsky

Library of Congress Cataloging-in-Publication Data
Goldberger, Paul.
Why architecture matters / Paul Goldberger.
    p. cm.
Includes bibliographical references and index.
ISBN 978-0-300-14430-7 (cloth : alk. paper)
1. Architecture—Psychological aspects. 2. Architecture and
society. I. Title.
NA2540.G63 2009
720.1′03—dc22   2009011071

A catalogue record for this book is available from the British
Library.

This paper meets the requirements of ANSI/NISO
Z39.48-1992 (Permanence of Paper).

10   9   8   7   6   5   4   3   2   1

also by paul goldberger

For Susan, Adam, Ben, and Alex;
Delphine, Thibeaux, and Josephine

and for Vincent Scully

contents

introduction

We could not live without architecture, but that is not why it matters. The purpose of this book is to explain what buildings do beyond keeping us out of the rain. Architecture may be able to stake a claim to being necessary to our lives in a way that poetry and literature and painting cannot, but the fact that buildings give us shelter is not the answer to the question posed by the title. If it were as simple as that, there would be nothing left to say.

Architecture begins to matter when it goes beyond protecting us from the elements, when it begins to say something about the world—when it begins to take on the qualities of art. You could say that architecture is what happens when people build with an awareness that they are doing something that reaches at least a little bit beyond the practical. It may be as tiny a gesture as painting the front door of a house red or as grand an undertaking as creating the rose window of a cathedral. It can be as casual as a sliver of decorative molding around a window or as carefully wrought as the ceiling of a Baroque church. A clapboard farm-house with a columned porch is architecture; so is a house by Frank Lloyd Wright in which every inch of every wall, every window, and every door is part of an elaborately considered composition. Wright liked to say that architecture began when he started building his sprawling modern houses on the American prairie; Mies van der Rohe said, more poetically and also more modestly, that the origin of architecture was in the first time "two bricks were put together well."

The making of architecture is intimately connected to the knowledge that buildings instill within us emotional reactions. They can make us feel and they can also make us think. Architecture begins to matter when it brings delight and sadness and perplexity and awe along with a roof over our heads. It matters when it creates serenity or exhilaration, and it matters just as much, I have to say, when it inspires anxiety, hostility, or fear. Buildings can do all of these things, and more. They represent social ideals; they are political statements; they are cultural icons. Architecture is surely our greatest physical symbol of the idea of community, our surest way to express in concrete form our belief in the notion of common ground. The way a community builds tells you, sometimes, all you need to know about its values: just to look at Radburn, New Jersey, will tell you that it is a suburb built to control the automobile, in the same way that it does not take long to figure out that Positano and the rest of the Amalfi Coast in Italy were built to connect to the sea. You can under-stand the difference between, say, the leafy precincts of Green-wich, Connecticut, and the suburban tracts of Levittown, Long

Island, more easily, I suspect, by comparing Greenwich's estates to Levittown's houses than you could by looking at the residents of each community. The people can mislead you more easily than their architecture can.

Buildings also stand as evidence of the power of memory. Who has not returned after many years to a house, a school, a hotel, or some other place in which meaningful events in your life occurred and not found that the buildings themselves unleashed a sense of the past too strong to ignore? Architectural historian Vincent Scully has said that architecture is a conversation between the generations, carried out across time, and while you could say that this is true of all forms of art and culture, in architecture the conversation is the most conspicuous, the most obvious, the most impossible to tune out. We may not all participate in the conversation, but we all have to listen to it. For that reason alone, architecture matters: because it is all around us, and what is all around us has to have an effect on us. That effect may be subtle and barely noticeable, or it may shake us to the core, but it will never fail to be there.

Because architecture is there, presenting itself to us even when we do not seek it out or even choose to be conscious of it, it makes sense to think about it in slightly different terms from the way in which we might discuss, say, Baroque music or Renaissance sculpture, which is to say that it makes sense to consider it not only in terms of great masterpieces but also in terms of everyday experience. Architecture is a part of daily life for everyone, whether or not they want it to be. You may visit Chartres Cathedral as a conscious act of intention, just as you might elect to read *Madame Bovary* or decide to hear a performance of Beethoven's late quartets, but you live your life within and around and beside dozens of other buildings, almost none of which you have chosen to be with. Some of them may be masterpieces and some of them may be the architectural equivalent of dime-store novels or elevator music. It is perfectly reasonable to talk about the meaning of literature without talking about Danielle Steel, but can you grapple with the impact of architecture without looking at Main Street?

I tend to think not, which is why the pages that follow will deal to a great extent with the everyday experience of looking at buildings, which is, for most people, a major reason—sometimes the only reason—that architecture matters. Masterpieces are no less important for this, and they will get plenty of attention here. It is not wrong to say that the greatest buildings provide the greatest moments of architectural experience. They certainly have for me. But I prefer to see architecture not as a sequential story of masterworks, a saga beginning with the Pyramids and the Parthenon and extending through Chartres and the Taj Mahal and the Duomo and the Laurentian Library and St. Paul's Cathedral, and then on to the work of Louis Sullivan and Wright and Le Corbusier and Mies van der Rohe, but as a continuum of cultural expression. Architecture "is the will of an epoch translated into space," Mies said. Buildings tell us what we are and what we want to be, and sometimes it is the average ones that tell us the most.

There are surely some readers for whom architecture matters in a more specific way than I have in mind here. For some, architecture matters because buildings are our greatest consumers of energy (far more than cars), and if we do not reduce the amount of energy consumed in constructing and maintaining our buildings, we will be in far worse shape than if every MINI Cooper owner traded in his car for a Hummer. I could not agree more with the urgency of the green architecture movement and with the wisdom as well as the practicality of making sustainable buildings. One of the most encouraging developments in the past decade is the extent to which the architectural profession has taken up the values of the environmental movement and made many of them its own. So I am in complete agreement with the move toward sustainable architecture, and I do not discuss it in this book only because my intention is to look at architecture from a broader and less technical standpoint. But there can be no doubt that one of the ways architecture continues to matter is in how it uses energy and that reducing the amount of energy consumed by buildings needs to be one of the highest priorities of our time.

By the same token, I am sure there are readers who feel that architecture matters because the building industry occupies a huge position in our economy and that if we can make it more efficient, the entire economy will benefit. For others, architecture matters because the technology of building is undergoing remarkable advances, allowing us to build all kinds of things that architects once could barely dream about. And there are surely readers who believe that architecture matters because people are in desperate need of housing and that architecture has the potential to address this as well as so many other urgent social needs. Here again, I am in agreement, and I do discuss the issue of the social responsibility of architecture in a limited way toward the end of chapter 1. But as with green architecture, the economics and technical aspects of building are not the focus of this book, however much I share a belief in their importance.

This book does not argue for a single theory of architecture, an all-encompassing worldview that can dictate form to the architect and explain it to the rest of us. I do not believe there is such a thing as a universal recipe for good architecture; even in ages with much more stylistic coherence than our own, there have always been a myriad of ways in which different architects have chosen to build. I am excited by the best architecture of any style and any period, and although the focus of this book is almost exclusively on Western architecture, what I say about space and symbol and form—and about the relation of everyday buildings to special ones—has application to architecture of all cultures. Architecture takes very different forms in different cultures, but the nature of our experience with such fundamental matters as proportion and scale and space and texture and materials and shapes and light is not as different as the appearance of the architecture itself may be. And it is the quest to understand these basic things that interests me the most—far more, surely, than any theory or dogma or cultural tradition that argues that there is a single acceptable way to build.

Architects, being artists, often see things differently, and they should: it probably helps to produce an important body of work if you believe that there is one true way. The blinders that theory represents can be useful, maybe even essential, to artists in the making of art. But I do not believe that they help the rest of us to appreciate and understand it.

But if not theory, what? What determines whether, to use Mies's phrase, the bricks are put together well? Why do some buildings lift the spirit and others depress it? Why are some buildings a joy and others painful? And why do some hardly register at all?

If there are many routes to the kingdom of architectural heaven, it does not mean that there are not still guideposts along the way. *Something* has to help us tell the good from the bad. Some of those guideposts are purely aesthetic: much proportion, for example, is based on the purity of the so-called Golden Section, the roughly three-by-five rectangle whose ratio of height to width is particularly pleasing to the eye, neither too bluntly square nor too elongated. We can analyze this and other combinations that make buildings pleasing as objects until we are blue in the face (and I will say something about such issues of visual perception in chapter 3), but such analyses will take us only so far. Ultimately architecture, though it can reach great aesthetic heights, achieves its meaning from the balance between aesthetic and other concerns. It must be understood as a complex and often contradictory set of conditions, in which art seeks to find some detente with the realities of the world. Architecture is always a response to limits—physical constraints, financial ones, or the demands of function. If it is seen purely as art or purely as a practical pursuit, it will never really be grasped.

In *Art [Objects]*, Jeanette Winterson asks how we can know the difference between art to be admired and art to be ignored. "Years ago, when I was living very briefly with a stockbroker who had a good cellar," she says, "I asked him how I could learn about wine.

" 'Drink it,' he said."

And so it is. Experience is not sufficient, but it is necessary. The only way to learn is to look, to look again, and then to look some more. If that does not guarantee connoisseurship in art any more than sampling a lot of wine can turn someone into a wine expert, it is the only possible beginning, and ultimately the most urgent part of the long process of learning. This book is firmly on the side of experience. Between walking the streets and reading a work of architectural history, I will always choose walking and the power of real perception. Facts—whether stylistic characteristics, names of obscure pieces of classical ornament, or the birthdates of great architects—can always be found later in books. The sense of being in architectural space—what it feels like, how it hits you in the eye and swirls around in your gut, and, if you are very lucky, sends shivers up your spine—cannot be understood except by being there.

Everything has a feel to it. Not just masterpieces but everything in the built world. The purpose of this book is to come to grips with how things feel to us when we stand before them, with how architecture affects us emotionally as well as intellectually. This book is not a work of architectural history or a guide to the styles or an architectural dictionary, though it contains elements of all three of these. Its most important message, I hope, is to encourage you to look, and to learn gradually how to trust your eye. Look for essences, not for superficial stylistic detail. Think about intentions, but do not be too forgiving on their behalf, for they have given birth to more bad architecture than good. As in art, intentions are necessary, but they are only a beginning, not an end in themselves. How good intentions become serious ideas which, in turn, inspire the creation of built form that is capable of pleasing us or, better still, of moving us, is the subject of the rest of this book.

1 meaning, culture, and symbol

There is no doubt whatever about the influence of architecture and structure upon human character and action. We make our buildings and afterwards they make us. They regulate the course of our lives.

WINSTON CHURCHILL

I know that architecture matters very much to me, but I have no desire to claim that it can save the world. Great architecture is not bread on the table, and it is not justice in the courtroom. It affects the quality of life, yes, and often with an astonishing degree of power. But it does not heal the sick, teach the ignorant, or in and of itself sustain life. At its best, it can help to heal and to teach by creating a comfortable and uplifting environment for these things to take place in. This is but one of the ways in which architecture, though it may not sustain life, can give the already sustained life meaning. When we talk about how architecture matters, it is important to understand that the way in which it matters—beyond, of course, the obvious fact of shelter—is the same way in which any kind of art matters: it makes life better.

Paradoxically, it is often the most mundane architecture that means the most to us—the roof over our heads, the random buildings that protect us from the rain and give us places to work and shop and sleep and be entertained. Buildings like these—the vernacular, the standard architectural language—are not the focus of this book, but I will discuss them because I reject the view that a clear line can be drawn between serious architecture and ordinary buildings. "A bicycle shed is a building, Lincoln Cathedral is architecture," wrote the art historian Sir Nikolaus Pevsner, but what of it? Both are buildings, both are architecture. Lincoln Cathedral is a vastly more complex and profound work of architecture than the bicycle shed, and it was created with more noble aspirations. But each structure has something to say about the culture that built it, each structure is of at least some interest visually, and each structure evokes certain feelings and emotions. There is much more to say about a great cathedral than about a generic shed, but each helps shape our environment. And the companions of the bicycle shed, the vernacular commercial and residential architecture of the mall and the highway strip and the suburban town of today, have a much greater impact on where we live than a distant cathedral.

Such buildings are not masterpieces, and woe to the politically correct critic who says they are. Yet we ignore them at our peril. McDonald's restaurants? Las Vegas casinos? Mobile homes and suburban tract houses and strip malls and shopping centers and office parks? They can be banal or they can be joyful and witty, but they are rarely transcendent. Yet they tell us much about who we are and about the places we want to make. And often they work well, galling as this is for most architecture critics to admit. Much of the built world in the United States is ugly, but then again, most of nineteenth-century London seemed ugly to Londoners, too. The artlessness of most of our built environment today probably reveals as much about us as the design of Paris or Rome revealed about the cultures that built those cities. What is certain is that it is impossible to think seriously about architecture today and not think about the built environment as a whole.

It is all connected and interdependent, from freeways to gardens, from shopping malls to churches and skyscrapers and gas stations. I have no desire to romanticize the landscape that surrounds us at the beginning of the twenty-first century, but I know that Pevsner's academic distinction no longer holds up.

Perhaps it never did, though there was surely a time when ordinary, everyday architecture seemed in many ways a simplified, scaled-down edition of great architecture, and the qualitative difference between the two was barely noticeable. Yes, the Georgian row house in London was more modest than the great country estate, but the two were of a kind; they spoke the same language, and even the simple slum houses seemed like stripped-down versions of the great house, bargain-basement offerings from the same catalogue. It is striking that it was such a relatively coherent architectural culture as that of London and other Western European cities that moved Pevsner to make his arbitrary and cold-hearted distinction between Architecture with a capital "A" and mere buildings, since the mere buildings of his experience in the early decades of the past century were far more ambitious as works of architecture than the mere buildings we see today. In eighteenth-century London, Georgian architecture created a language, and out of that language of architectural elements both ordinary buildings and masterpieces could be made. If you were an architect you understood the language well and could write in it; if you were an educated layman, you could recognize and appreciate its details. But if you lacked any knowledge at all, you could still take pleasure in the clarity and the rhythm of the buildings constructed in that language, and you could see the way it created a city of lively beauty.

We need not speak only of London or of Europe. In nineteenth- and early-twentieth-century New York, for example, there was a quality to the brownstones that lined the side streets, and to the Georgian- and Renaissance-inspired apartment buildings that later lined the avenues, and even to the cramped and fetid tenements, that also suggested a common architectural language. It was a language of masonry, redolent with ornament and detail, emerging from the belief that every building, no matter how private, showed a public presence—that it had an obligation to the street and to anyone who passed before it, whether or not they had reason to walk through its doors. A language of scale was shared by the buildings that together formed the streets of New York in the hundred years from the mid-nineteenth century to the mid-twentieth; though the buildings were often large, they were oriented to the pedestrian and connected to one another as elements along a street—elements of a larger whole, not primarily objects in themselves. This common language reflected a respect for background, for the notion that buildings create an urban fabric, and from that comes the beginning of a civilized environment.

It is odd to think of the decorated cornice on a Ninth Avenue tenement as a gesture of civilization, but in the cityscape of New York at the end of the nineteenth century, it surely was. That cornice engages the eye, connects the building to its neighbors visually, and makes it part of the larger composition of the street.

And it suggests that a building has some purpose other than merely keeping its occupants out of the rain—to say that it exists, in however a meager, awkward, even vulgar way, to enrich the city around it. It makes gestures to you and to me, even if we never have any connection to it other than walking by.

That intention, the way in which the tenement was clearly intended to enrich the street and therefore the life of the city, is what makes Pevsner's distinction less than useful today. Is the decorated tenement simply a fancy bicycle shed? Or is it an earthbound echo of Lincoln Cathedral? An improved ape or a damaged angel? The tenement is a practical construction designed to be more than merely practical, and—leaving value judgments aside—that is as good a definition of architecture as I can imagine.

By that standard, of course, virtually every building is architecture, so long as its physical form reflects some degree of civilizing intent. The intent may reveal itself in something as modest as the crude curlicues of the tenement cornice or as intricate and profound as the stonework and stained glass of Chartres or the space of Borromini's extraordinary church of Sant'Ivo in Rome. Architectural intent is not merely a matter of decoration, though it can be; it can emerge from the conscious crafting of space, the deliberate shaping of form, or the juxtaposition of well-considered materials. Art is defined largely by intention, and so is architecture.

Architecture is balanced, precisely and precariously, between art and practicality. These needs do not precede art and they do not follow it; they are not subservient to it and they are not superior to it. Each aspect of architecture coexists, and every work of architecture must to a greater or lesser degree take them all into account. Vitruvius, writing in ancient Rome around 30 BC, set out the three elements of architecture as "commodity, firmness, and delight," and no one has done better than his tripartite definition, for it cogently sums up the architectural paradox: a building must be useful while at the same time it must be the opposite of useful, since art—delight, in Vitruvian parlance—by its very essence has no mundane function. And then, on top of all of that, a building must be constructed according to the laws of engineering, which is to say that it must be built to stand up.

Vitruvius presents these conflicting realities of architecture not as a paradox but as a matter of coexistence; his point is to remind us that a building must simultaneously be useful, well built and visually appealing. Neither does Vitruvius explicitly rank the three elements in order of importance. While it can be pleasing to think of them in ascending significance, this is a subtle footnote to the real message that Vitruvius conveys, which is that they are interdependent. Without firmness and delight, commodity is nothing. But delight needs firmness, not only so the building stands up, but also so its art can reach its greatest heights. The builders of the Pyramids, the Greek temples, Roman aqueducts, and Gothic cathedrals were all engineers as much as architects; to them these disciplines were one. So, too, with Brunelleschi and his Duomo in Florence, or Michelangelo at St. Peter's. In our time, the disciplines have diverged, and engineers are not architects. But every great structure of modern times, from Jorn Utzon's Sydney Opera House to Frank Gehry's Guggenheim Museum Bilbao, is a product of engineers as much as of architects; without firmness, there will be no delight. All three elements of architecture are essential.

So architecture is art and it is not art; it is art and it is something more, or less, as the case may be. This is its paradox and its glory, and always has been: art and not art, at once. Architecture is not like a painting or a novel or a poem; its role is to provide shelter, and its reality in the physical world makes it unlike anything else that we commonly place in the realm of art. Unlike a symphony, a building must fulfill a certain practical function—giving us a place to work, or to live, or to shop or to worship or to be entertained—and it must stand up. But a building is not at all like other things that we place in the realm of the practical but that may have aesthetic aspirations, such as an airplane, an automobile, or a cooking pot. For we expect a work of architecture, when it succeeds in its aesthetic aims, to be capable of creating a more profound set of feelings than a well-designed toaster.

Sir John Soane's Museum, the architect's extraordinary townhouse in London—and one of the greatest works by an architect who was one of the most brilliant and original design forces to have come out of Georgian London—contains a room that can make this clear. It was Soane's breakfast room, and it is fairly small, with a round table set under a low dome that is not a real dome but a canopy, supported by narrow columns at four corners. Where the canopy meets the corners, Soane placed small, round mirrors, so that the occupants of the breakfast table can see one another without looking directly at each other. The yellowish walls are lined with bookcases and paintings, and natural light tumbles in softly beside the canopy, indirectly, from above. Soane liked to create rooms within rooms and spaces that connect in unusual ways with other spaces, and in the breakfast room you can see that he is doing it not just as the early-nineteenth-century's version of razzle-dazzle but to provide a kind of psychic comfort. The dome is protecting, but it is not quite enclosing, a reminder that while we may feel uncommunicative and vulnerable early in the morning, we need to move out of that stage into the world. The breakfast room functions as a kind of halfway house, cozy in a way that other, more formal spaces tend not to be, and soft in the way it introduces us to the day. It is a room of great beauty and serenity, perfectly balanced between openness and enclosure, between public and private. The British architecture critic Ian Nairn was exaggerating only somewhat when he called the breakfast room "probably the deepest penetration of space and of man's position in space, and hence in the world, that any architect has ever created."

In the breakfast room, Soane used architecture to fulfill a routine function and create a powerful, almost transcendent experience at the same time. For me there are other buildings, too, that achieve the extraordinary as they fulfill a function that, in and of itself, is perfectly ordinary. In 1929, when Mies van der Rohe was asked to create a small pavilion to represent Germany at the world exposition in Barcelona, he produced a sublime composition of glass, marble, steel, and concrete, arranged to appear almost as if the elements were flat planes floating in space. The white, flat roof and the walls of green marble with stainless

Sir John Soane, breakfast room, Sir John Soane's Museum, London

steel columns in front of them combine to have immense sensual power, a tiny exhibit pavilion in which you feel an entire world of continuous, floating space, and one of the first modern buildings anywhere to convey a sense of richness and luxury amid great restraint—a building that in some ways has more in common, at least spiritually, with the spare classical architecture of Japan.

The Great Workroom of the Johnson Wax Administration Building in Racine, Wisconsin, designed by Frank Lloyd Wright

Mies van der Rohe, Barcelona Pavilion

and finished a decade later, in 1939, had an even more mundane purpose, which was to house clerical employees. Wright created an enormous, altogether spectacular room of light and swirling curves under a translucent ceiling. The room was lined in brick with clerestory windows of translucent Pyrex tubes, and its structure was supported on a forest of slender, tapering columns, each of which was topped by a huge, round disc, like a lily pad of concrete floating in the translucent ceiling. The space looks, even now, like a futurist fantasy; it must have been altogether astonishing in the 1930s. While Wright's specially designed typing chairs and steel worktables were less than functional and the room, though awash in natural light, allowed no views to the exterior—this was Frank Lloyd Wright's world you were in, and not for an instant would he let you forget it—the Johnson Wax building still gave typists a modern cathedral, an ennobling place, in which to work.

Frank Lloyd Wright, Great Workroom, Johnson Wax headquarters, Racine, Wisconsin

Another example, quite different, but worth discussing in more detail, since it is perhaps the building where, at least in the United States, architectural form and symbol come together with a more serene grace than in any other: the original campus of the University of Virginia at Charlottesville, by Thomas Jefferson. Designed when Jefferson was seventy-four, the "academical village," as he liked to call it, consists of two parallel rows of five classical houses, called pavilions, connected by low, colonnaded walkways, which face each other across a wide, magnificently proportioned grassy lawn. At the head of the lawn, presiding over the entire composition, is the Rotunda, a domed structure he based on the Pantheon in Rome.

Each pavilion is designed according to a different classical motif, so that together they constitute a virtual education in classical architecture: the directness and simplicity of the Doric order, the richness of the Corinthian, can here be compared in what amounts to a Jeffersonian fugue of classical variations. As Jefferson conceived it, the Rotunda served as the library, which was a splendid piece of symbolism, for it turned the form used to honor the ancient gods into a temple of the book and then gave that temple pride of place in the composition.

There are other kinds of symbolism, too: the pavilions, with their great stylistic range, stand as a kind of beginning of the American tendency to pick and choose from history, shaping the styles of the past to our own purposes. And the pavilions (which originally housed the faculty) and the students' rooms set behind, connected by colonnaded walkways, meant that the university lived together as a community.

The whole place is a lesson, not just in the didactic sense of the classical orders, but in a thousand subtler ways as well. Ultimately the University of Virginia is an essay in balance—balance between the built world and the natural one, between the individual and the community, between past and present, between order and freedom. There is order to the buildings, freedom to the lawn itself—but as the buildings order and define and enclose the great open space, so does the space make the buildings sensual and rich. Neither the buildings nor the lawn would have any meaning without the other, and the dialogue they enter into is a sublime composition.

The lawn is terraced, so that it steps down gradually as it moves away from the Rotunda, adding a whole other rhythm to

Thomas Jefferson, the Lawn, University of Virginia, Charlottesville

the composition. The lawn is a room, and the sky its ceiling; I know of few other outdoor places anywhere where the sense of architectural space can be so intensely felt.

In Jefferson's buildings, there are other kinds of balances as well—between the icy coolness of the white-painted stone and the warm redness of the brick, between the sumptuousness of the Corinthian order and the restraint of the Doric, between the rhythms of the columns, marching on and on down the lawn, and the masses of the pavilions. In the late afternoon light all this can tug at your heart, and you feel that you can touch that light, dancing on those columns, making the brick soft and rich. There is awesome beauty here, but also utter clarity. It becomes clear that Jefferson created both a total abstraction and a remarkably literal expression of an idea. Architecture has rarely been as sure of itself, as creative, as inventive, and as relaxed as it is here.

We certainly could not live with constant attention to music and would surely tune out even the loveliest sounds if we were surrounded by them at every moment, as we are by architecture. Because architecture is omnipresent, it obliges us to stop seeing it. We cannot take it in constantly at its highest level of intensity, as we have seen. And yet we cannot not take it in, either. All architecture, from art at its highest to the architecture that barely makes it over the threshold of intention, shapes the world in which we live most of our lives. With one foot necessarily in the real world, it straddles the gap between reality and dreams. To be engaged with architecture is to be engaged with almost everything else as well: culture, society, politics, business, history, family, religion, education. Every building exists to house something, and what it houses is itself part of the pursuit of architecture. The joy of architecture as art is only an aspect of the experience of architecture, profound though it may be; there is also great satisfaction to understanding the built environment as a form of engagement with every other function imaginable.

Architecture is social as well as individual: as it exists in physical reality, it exists in social reality, too. Two people can experience a work of architecture as differently as they can experience a painting or a symphony, but the way architecture enforces social interaction, imposing a common experience despite the possible differences in judgment that may result, is unique. It takes many people to make a work of architecture and many people to use one. The novel may reach its fullest meaning when read by a single person, acting alone; but the concert hall or museum or office building or even private house derives much of its meaning from the social acts that occur within it and from how its physical form is intricately involved in those social acts. When we see a concert hall empty, after hours, we can appreciate its physical form, but we see it as a vacuum, cut off from its purpose, and thus we barely see it at all. Even a cathedral—which architectural pilgrims are most likely to visit at quiet times and which may confer extraordinary gifts of intimacy on the solitary visitor—rises to yet another level of meaning when we experience it filled with worshipers.

Architecture is the ultimate physical representation of a culture, more so than even its flag. The White House, the Capitol, the Houses of Parliament, the Pyramids, the Eiffel Tower, the Brandenburg Gate, St. Basil's Cathedral, the Sydney Opera House, the Empire State Building, the Golden Gate Bridge. The list could expand to thousands of structures, and they need not be celebrated ones; county courthouses and town halls in small communities everywhere can possess the same qualities and convey the same meaning: architecture is a powerful icon because it represents common experience, more so than any other art, and resonates more than most other aspects of common cultural experience. A flag is a relatively simple object whose entire effect lies in its blunt, direct, and total symbolism, but architecture functions as a different kind of icon. It is complicated, experienced over time, and generally large enough to be perceived in very different ways by different people, however much they may share a commitment to its iconic status. Every work of architecture, whatever its symbolic associations, also exists as an aesthetic experience, as pure physical sensation. The White House is four walls, a portico, some severe Georgian detailing, and some splendid rooms full of elegant objects and decoration, and while only a Martian unaware of its history could perceive it only as a pure object, no one can perceive it only as pure symbol, either. Every iconic piece of architecture speaks to us simultaneously as both form and symbol.

When a work of architecture functions as icon, then it matters in a different kind of way from other buildings. The power of architectural icons is undiminished today, even as so many other symbols of our culture appear to weaken. We can see this not only in the continued magnetic pull of such places as the White House and the Capitol—a pull that seems undiminished by the cynicism with which voters regard the occupants of these buildings and the political events that go on inside them—but also in the ascension to iconic status of the World Trade Center after its destruction on September 11, 2001, when tragic circumstances led the United States to embrace, surely for the first time, an enormous, modernist, commercial building and confer on it all of the symbolic meaning that is often reserved for more traditional kinds of architecture. (For years after September 11, sidewalk vendors in New York were selling pictures of the World Trade Center in the way that they once sold pictures of Malcolm X or Martin Luther King, Jr.) That it took martyrdom to render the Twin Towers beloved and to make people view them as being as fundamentally an American symbol as the Lincoln Memorial is not surprising, of course, not only because Americans have always had a certain conflict with modernism—we want to be seen as advanced, indeed as the most advanced culture there is, but at the same time we have always been most comfortable keeping one foot in the past, like Jefferson seeking to move forward by adopting and reinventing what has come before, not by breaking with tradition. For many Americans, before September 11, Colonial Williamsburg probably felt like a more natural symbol of the country than did a very tall box of glass and steel.

The risks of breaking with history were clear in the saga surrounding another important icon, the work of architecture that is probably the first modernist civic monument to achieve any degree of iconic status in the United States: the Vietnam Veterans Memorial in Washington, D.C., by Maya Lin, completed in 1981. This is also worth discussing in detail, since it is an extraordinary story, and not only because Lin was a twenty-one-year-old student when she designed it. When the jury of an architectural competition selected Lin's design—a pair of two-hundred-foot-long black granite walls that join to form a V which embraces a gently sloping plot of ground—what troubled many people was not Lin's age but her reliance on abstraction. Where were the statues, where were the traditional symbols? The fact that Lin proposed to give the memorial a sense of immediacy and connection to the dead by carving the names of all 57,692 Americans who were killed in Vietnam from 1963 to 1973 into the granite did not seem, to some people, sufficient to remove it from what they considered the realm of cold, impersonal abstraction. The project went ahead only after a compromise led to the addition of a statue of soldiers and a flagpole at some distance from the wall. But once the memorial was built, it turned out to be Lin's original design—the wall of names—that possesses the real emotional power, not the mawkish, literalizing elements added for fear the wall would not speak clearly enough. The latter have turned out to be superfluous to the original design, which appears to speak more clearly to great numbers of people than any other abstract work in the United States today.

By traditional measures the Vietnam Veterans Memorial is not architecture at all—it has no roof, no doors, no interior. It does not pretend to be a building. But it employs the techniques of architecture to what can only be called the highest and most noble civic purpose, and does so more successfully than almost anything else built in our age. Indeed, it stands, quite simply, as the most important evidence the late twentieth century produced that design can still serve as a unifying social force.

At the Vietnam Veterans Memorial, monumentality creates a true public realm, public not only in the sense of ownership but also in that of intellectual and emotional connection. The memorial is public, people feel, because it is about them, and its physical form touches their souls. This memorial has the power to move people of startlingly different backgrounds and political views, and it performs this difficult task of making common experience when society seems infinitely fragmented. This work of architecture provides common ground.

The wide V shape of the wall is subtly sited: one arm of the wall points toward the Washington Monument, the other to the Lincoln Memorial, tying the memorial—and by implication the

Maya Lin, Vietnam Veterans Memorial, Washington, D.C.

tragedy of Vietnam—to the landmarks of official Washington, and hence to the epic of our history. The memorial is not conspicuous from afar, since it does not rise much above ground level at all: it may be one of the few great architectural works anywhere whose approach is marked only by directional signs, not by a glimpse of the thing itself. You approach through the Mall, the monumental axial green space of Washington, which recedes into the background as the wall becomes visible, just a sliver at first, and then larger. It is not huge, and at the beginning, where it is just a thin slice of granite connected to the ground, it seems tiny. As you walk beside it and the ground descends, the wall grows in height; more and more names of the dead appear, chronologically listed, until suddenly the wall begins to loom large and there is a sense that you have gone deeper into the abyss of war as you descend further into the ground and Washington itself disappears. Then, as you turn the corner at the center of the memorial, you begin to move slowly back upward again, toward the light, the sun, and the city—and you realize that, metaphorically at least, you have undergone a passage toward redemption.

Literal honor to the dead through the presence of their names; metaphorical representation of the war as a descent from which the nation rose again; symbolic connections to the larger world. What more could we ask? There is beauty here, and room for each of us to think our own thoughts, and the brilliance of a design that reminds us at every moment that private loss and public tragedy are irrevocably joined.

Monuments as powerful, as subtle, and as successful at appealing to a wide range of people as the Vietnam Veterans Memorial are rare in any period. All buildings have some symbolic meaning, however, even if it is more conventional and more common than the symbolism of a great memorial, and the question worth asking is how effectively does a piece of architecture carry out its symbolic role—how well does it communicate whatever message it may have that goes beyond the purely functional, beyond even the aesthetic appeal of its physical form? Frank Lloyd Wright, for all his determination to reinvent the form of the single-family house, was passionately devoted to the very traditional idea of the house as a symbol of the nuclear family, and almost all of his houses had large fireplaces, either as the dominant elements of the main living space or set off in inglenooks of their own, all to emphasize the connection between home and hearth. (Wright liked to present himself as a radical outsider, but he was less interested in changing society than in changing architecture, and he tended to believe that the best way to keep the American agrarian, family tradition strong was to house it in new architectural form created specifically for the American continent rather than transported from elsewhere. It was a case of radical art for a more conservative end than Wright wanted people to believe.)

Think, for a moment, about another of the most common building types, the bank. Once, most American banks tended to be serious, classically inspired buildings, civic presences symbolizing both the stature of the bank in a community and protection for the hoard of cash within. Who would doubt that their money is safer in a limestone temple or an Italian Renaissance palazzo than in a storefront? Traditional architectural style served a powerful symbolic purpose here, in the same way it always has in religious buildings.

Today, banks are vast national or international corporate enterprises, not local ones, and most cash exists electronically. How do you create an architectural expression for the protection of blips on a computer screen? Surely not by building a replica of a Greek temple on Main Street. And cash itself now is generally dispensed not from a bank vault but from an ATM, a vending machine device that demands no architectural expression at all, save for a wall onto which it can be installed.

I mention all of this not to say what banks should or should not look like, and certainly not to deny that there is still great symbolic power present in some of the fine old banks that previous generations have handed down to us, but to underscore how social and technological change affects architectural meaning. A grand and sumptuous classical bank may still give pleasure as a monumental artifact, but that is about all; customers in it today are not likely to feel the sense of protection that the building was intended to give, largely because they no longer need or seek such protection in an age of electronic banking. We may even feel a greater sense of emotion in experiencing the glory of an old bank as a piece of monumental architecture than previous generations did in experiencing it as a place of safety and security—but that is beside the point. Even if we find the old bank exhilarating, it has a different meaning as a work of architecture now than before. (And it often has a very different function, too. In New York, several of the city's finest old banks have been converted into catering halls, party spaces which underscore that the buildings now exist for pleasure, not necessity.)

So how, then, does one design a bank today? The "icon," or symbol on the computer screen, that Microsoft Money uses to denote that its online banking system is working is a line moving back and forth between a miniature house and a miniature classical temple—data being transferred from home to bank, or vice versa. No one looking at such a screen could doubt what those icons represent, and they stand as confirmation that the symbolic power of the classical bank remains a part of collective memory, and hence still has practical application, even in an age in which the traditional function of the bank has changed altogether.

But is this a sign of weakness or of strength? Does the fact that the classical bank has been reduced to the status of an icon on a computer screen confirm its continued vitality as a symbol or make it no more than a cartoon? Something of both, I suspect. But what the computer icon really proves is that our age has not yet been able to create any architectural image for the bank that is nearly as potent as the traditional one. We still use the classical bank when we need to create an image that says "bank," even though we do not use the classical bank much any more when we want to make a real bank because it has so little connection to the realities of how banking is done.

Occasionally banks are built today that self-consciously evoke the monumental grandeur of the old classical ones. But their designs, however well meaning, cannot be the same as the ones that have survived from the late nineteenth and early twentieth centuries, for classical banks built in an age of cyberspace become, in effect, exercises in nostalgia. They do not emerge from the conditions that gave birth to the great bank buildings of the past, when cash needed physical protection and society understood and respected the idea that a bank was the architectural expression of that act of protection. Today, building that kind of old-fashioned bank may represent an earnest yearning for that time, but it is unlikely to be convincing in the way that a surviving older bank is. Yearning is rarely enough to confer architectural meaning on its own, which is why such buildings often end up as three-dimensional versions of the computer icon—cartoons built of stone.

This is not to deny the complexity of the problem of creating a decent, appealing architecture that expresses the conditions of the moment. When banking is less and less a matter of tangible goods—that is, cash—it is less and less easy to give it meaningful architectural representation. Not for nothing have even great banking institutions come to look more and more like offices and branch banks more like storefronts, and even the ones that work reasonably well have given up on almost any level of architectural ambition. Of course, this is fitting symbolism in itself: the reality is a certain banality, much as the great architectural critic Lewis Mumford noted half a century ago when he reviewed the United Nations headquarters and observed that the most conspicuous element of the complex was not a tower or an assembly hall but the Secretariat skyscraper, a perfect symbol, Mumford said, of the triumph of the bureaucracy. So, too, are banks as storefront offices and ATMs perfect symbols of the evolution of banking away from the real—cash—and to the virtual world of electronic transactions.

When Vitruvius, writing in ancient Rome, dictated that architecture should provide "commodity, firmness, and delight," he also said that architecture was, in effect, the beginning of civilization and that all other arts and fields of study connected to it and were descended from it—an observation that, as architectural historian Fil Hearn wrote in *Ideas That Shaped Buildings,* "offered the art of building perhaps the highest encomium it has ever received," rendering the architect, in effect, the keeper of civilization. (Vitruvius's work consisted of ten sections and included long discussions about the classical orders, about the proper way to build temples, amphitheaters, and houses, and about materials and the siting of cities.)

But if Vitruvius can be considered the beginning, or the foundation, of architectural theory, it was a foundation with not much built upon it for more than fifteen hundred years. In the Middle Ages, great engineer-architects built some of the most extraordinary structures that have ever existed, but they did not codify their ideas into long treatises, as Vitruvius had done. The notion that one could prescribe in words an ideal way of building, and a purpose for architecture, returned in the Renaissance, when Vitruvius was rediscovered and used as a model for an updated treatise by Leon Battista Alberti in the middle of the fifteenth century. Alberti urged a return to a classical architecture based on the buildings of ancient Rome, not just because he found classicism aesthetically appealing, but because he believed that in building correctly lay virtue. "Alberti felt impelled to cite the benefits to society of beautiful, well-planned buildings: they give pleasure; they enhance civic pride; they confer dignity and honor on the community; if sacred, they encourage piety; and they may even move an enemy to refrain from damaging them," Fil Hearn has written, noting that Alberti also observed that the architect had the potential to affect national security as much as a general and to improve his country as much as an artist. Alberti seems to have had as pure and natural an understanding of the balance between aesthetics and practical, not to say political, matters as any architect ever has. He celebrated the artistic side of architecture and claimed that architecture owed more to painting than to anything else. Yet he ranked mathematics as nearly as important and proposed precise, mathematical explanations of proportion. And he understood the relation between architecture and power as clearly as Machiavelli.

It is hard to overestimate Alberti's importance. In an essay in the *New Yorker,* the art historian Joseph Connors summed up Alberti with precision and elegance, writing that out of his "mixture of erudition, logic and experience came prescient ideas that would transform architecture. Beauty is not the same as ornament. The beautiful is that which cannot be changed except for the worse; a beautiful building is one to which nothing can be added and from which nothing can be taken away. Modest materials arranged in proportionate relationships are more likely to be beautiful than rich materials badly arranged. The eye can perceive harmony just like the ear. Churches should be austere and dark; shadows induce a sense of sacred fear and the finest ornament in a place of worship is a flame. Palace planning should reflect degrees of distance between the ruler and his subjects. The house is like a small city, and the city a large house. Nature delights in the measure and the mean, and so should the architect. Beauty has the power to disarm the raging barbarian; there is no greater security against violence and injury than beauty and dignity."

Alberti may have erred on the side of earnestness, not to say naïveté, in his confidence that architectural beauty could protect a civilization—his Machiavellian pragmatism seems to have been limited to the process of making buildings, not to their effects. Still, I am not sure there has ever been a more elegant and concise set of architectural directions. Alberti's writing inspired numerous other odes to classicism, most famously the *Four Books of Architecture,* by Andrea Palladio, the great sixteenth-century builder of Italian country villas. Palladio presented his own work as evidence of his theoretical ideas, thus beginning the practice of architects writing books in which they attempt to articulate ideal ways of building and then show their own buildings, presumably as a demonstration of these ideal notions. Palladio's treatise was as important as his buildings in establishing him as a central figure in Western architecture and in giving us the adjective "Palladian" to attach to a certain kind of symmetrical, classically inspired villa, generally with a pedimented temple front.

The notion that there is a right way to build—morally and ethically, that is, not structurally—is really the basis of most architectural theory that has followed. In England, A. W. N. Pugin in the

1830s and 1840s argued that Gothic, not classical, architecture was the road to civic good, social virtue, and, most important, godliness. For Pugin, an intense Roman Catholic, Gothic was the only true religious architecture, period. He worked with Charles Barry, the architect of the Houses of Parliament, and designed most of the interiors and much of the architectural detail in Parliament, but beyond working on this building and designing a few of his own, Pugin played a major role as a theorist in creating the Gothic Revival. It is no exaggeration to say that the close connection between the Gothic style and churches that still exists today is due in large part to forces Pugin helped set in motion. (Say "church," and it is highly likely that something at least loosely resembling Gothic architecture will come into your mind.) Pugin was aided by John Ruskin, whose long treatises *The Seven Lamps of Architecture* and *The Stones of Venice,* surely the most ambitious architectural writing since Palladio, extended the argument beyond architecture's influence over what we might call the external morality of society into the idea that there is also a morality within a structure itself. Ruskin said that Gothic architecture, by virtue of the fact that it was honest, clear, and direct in its use of structure and materials, had a whole other kind of morality to it, beyond that conferred by its traditions and its close connection to the church. Nature, Ruskin thought, provided the proper model for building. "An architect should live as little in our cities as a painter," Ruskin wrote. "Send him to our hills, and let him study there what nature understands by a buttress, and what by a dome." To Ruskin, not only structure but every material used in building had its own integrity, which dictated how it should be properly used, a notion that would come to be particularly important to modernist architects. He disliked surface decoration and argued for plain, workaday buildings for ordinary purposes, and he believed that real architecture—which is to say Gothic-style architecture—should be reserved for noble, civic, or sacred purpose.

Most buildings, of course, were not designed to demonstrate theories, and in the late nineteenth century, many architects who designed Gothic-style buildings did so because they were the fashion, and that was enough. The concept that there was some sort of moral integrity to "honest" structure did not hold water with most architects, and all kinds of buildings were produced in all kinds of styles, many of the best of them having nothing whatsoever to do with these ideas. Decoration, harmonious proportions, comfortable scale were all notions that were only occasionally connected to structural honesty, but to many architects, they meant a lot more. The architect and critic Russell Sturgis wrote that the typical public building was designed to be "a box with a pretty inside, put into another box with a pretty outside," and never mind any rational connection between the two. Still, Ruskin's writing had considerable influence. It led directly to what became known as the Arts and Crafts movement in Britain, led by William Morris, which called for a revival of craftsmanship, something it saw as closely connected to the principles of honesty and directness that Ruskin believed gave buildings integrity. Ruskin's notion that there is such a thing as a building itself being moral or inherently honest was picked up by Eugène-Emmanuel Viollet-le-Duc, a French theorist who carried it still further and argued that architecture had an obligation to be rational. Viollet-le-Duc, too, was taken by Gothic architecture and saw honesty rather than mystery in it. His case for structural rationality set out the beginning tenets of what would become the underlying argument of almost every modern architect.

Some, like the Viennese architect Adolf Loos, whose most famous essay was called "Ornament and Crime," took Viollet-le-Duc's theory to the next level and put the issue of morality back on the table. Decoration was not only misguided and old-fashioned, Loos said, it was immoral, and he argued for an austere architecture as the only form of design suitable to the modern age. The great French-Swiss architect Le Corbusier, in *Towards a New Architecture* and *When the Cathedrals Were White,* as well as the Italian futurist Antonio Sant'Elia and the German architect Walter Gropius, saw the machine as the great inspiration of the age and urged architects to follow it, not by making their designs literally machinelike, but by giving them the directness and lack of extraneous elements that characterized machines. They were not troubled by the fact that the notion that a building had an obligation to be direct and clear in its structure—to reveal itself, so to speak, rather than to hide itself behind the clutter of decoration—had actually emerged out of the architectural theory of Gothicists like Ruskin and Viollet-le-Duc and was not in and of itself an argument for designing buildings that would not look like anything that had come before. But it became one, as modernists used these notions to create a rationale for rejecting history and designing as if with a clean slate. Sigfried Giedion would attempt to give all of this further justification in his epic work *Space, Time and Architecture: The Growth of a New Tradition,* published in 1941, which argued that a cool, austere, somewhat abstract modernism was the culmination of the history of Western architecture. To Giedion, the architectural past was, quite literally, prologue, and he saw architectural history as a straight line pointing inevitably toward the modernist architecture of the twentieth century.

Curiously, Frank Lloyd Wright, who would ultimately be identified more with his claims that the flowing, open, horizontal space of his "Prairie Houses" and other buildings represented the expression of a quintessentially American impulse, also made similar arguments about the machine, and even before the Europeans did. In a remarkable lecture called "The Art and Craft of the Machine," delivered at Jane Addams's Hull House in Chicago in 1901, Wright talked about Gutenberg, the inventor of movable type, and made the extraordinary observation that the printed book was, in a sense, the first machine and that its arrival profoundly changed architecture. It was not the printing press itself that Wright was calling a machine, it was the book. He owed, and acknowledged, a certain debt in this point, of course, to Victor Hugo, who made a somewhat similar observation in *The Hunchback of Notre Dame,* but Wright's way of expressing this point was very much his own. Before printed books, Wright said, "all the intellectual forces of the people converged to one point—architecture. Down to the fifteenth century the chief register of humanity is architecture." Wright referred to the most important pieces of architecture as "great granite books" and said that "down to the time of Gutenberg architecture is the principal writing—the universal writing of humanity." But with the arrival of printing, Wright said, "Human thought discovers a mode of perpetuating itself still more simple and easy. Architecture is dethroned. Gutenberg's letters of lead are about to supersede Orpheus's letters of stone. The book is about to kill the edifice," he concluded, here reworking Hugo's phrase literally.

Wright's theory ignores the oral tradition of literature, which allowed words to become part of cultural history even before the invention of the printing press. Like almost everything Wright wrote, this lecture is wildly overstated, full of Whitmanesque hyperbole. But for all of that, it remains an astonishing observation, for in a way it is the beginning of the modern connection between media and architecture. Wright was acting on the presumption that architecture was a form of communication, a radical thought indeed for 1901—architecture as media. "The Art and Craft of the Machine," then, can be viewed as an early example—perhaps *the* early example—of the notion of architecture as media, which today, when we think of almost everything in terms of its implications for information technology, is astonishing. Wright was viewing architecture as a system by which the culture preserved and extended itself—in fact, as the primary system by which the culture did this, since Wright saw art and sculpture as subsidiary to architecture, as merely tools in its arsenal of communication. Sometimes buildings literally did tell stories (the iconography of the Gothic cathedrals is the most potent example), although I imagine Wright was thinking not only in such literal terms but also about the architectural experience itself, as well as about the notion that the creation of structure and space was a form of communication and a way of conveying cultural values between the generations. Now, as I said, architecture was not the only system of preserving culture, as Wright would have had us believe, but there is no question that it was a very powerful one, and Wright's notion that the power of architecture was diminished by the way in which the printing press allowed an alternative means for ideas to become widely disseminated stands as an extraordinary moment in the evolution of thinking about the purpose of architecture.

Wright went on to say that architecture had been so weakened by invention of the printing press that architects felt there was little to do beyond copying the styles of the past and that only now, with the coming of modern architecture, was the field of architecture in a position to resume its former role as a central pursuit in society. Wright's notion that everything between the Gothic cathedrals and the twentieth century was an architectural wasteland is absurd, of course. But he did identify an issue that remains as sharp a sign of division today as ever, which is the question of how important it is for architects to invent something new, and that even if you do not consider reusing an architectural style from the past to be immoral, as Wright and the other modernists did, is it nevertheless a lesser pursuit than designing something new and different? Is there such a thing as a "style for the time," as modernists liked to say?

Most architectural theories of modern times, as throughout history, have been attempts to justify a particular style. Ruskin, Morris, and Wright, for all they talked of architecture as being determined by moral principles and of its critical role as an exemplar of society's aims, were no exceptions. Aesthetics, and the wish that buildings look a particular way, almost always provided the underlying, if sometimes unspoken, rationale behind architectural theory. Ruskin all but admitted this when he said, "Taste is the only morality. Tell me what you like and I'll tell you what you are."

But if we are thinking about what architecture means in our culture, the discussion cannot begin and end with aesthetics. What of the purpose of architecture in solving social problems, in housing the poor, in creating civilized environments for teaching and learning? Don't architects have a responsibility to make the world better, as Vitruvius and Alberti would remind us? Does an ugly public housing project that provides a home for fifty families not serve a larger purpose than a more attractive one that gives only twenty families a roof over their heads? Wasn't it the job of architects to try and solve the problem of rebuilding New Orleans after Hurricane Katrina?

The answer is yes, and no. When the professional expertise of architects can provide answers to social problems that would otherwise not be found, as in creating attractive, buildable, affordable housing in New Orleans, or in designing viable temporary housing after an earthquake, or in figuring out a way to lay out a school or a hospital to maximize the satisfaction it will give to the people who use it, then architecture is fulfilling a social responsibility. But architects are not makers of public policy, and while they can design whatever they please, they can build only what a client wants to pay for. It is not the architect's role to solve the problem of housing the poor. It is the architect's role to give the poor the very best housing possible when society decides that it is ready to address this urgent problem. The same applies for education and health care and every other social need that can be satisfied, in part, by more and better buildings: it is the job of architects to design the best buildings, the most beautiful and civilized and useful ones, but society must be willing to address these problems before the architect can do his or her best work. In *Complexity and Contradiction in Architecture,* Robert Venturi's seminal work of theory, published in 1966—a book that is preoccupied primarily with aesthetics and is a potent and eloquent attack on the stark simplicity of much modernist architecture—Venturi took note of the rising tide of demands in the 1960s that architects assume a broader role. "The architect's ever diminishing power and his growing ineffectualness in shaping the whole environment can perhaps be reversed, ironically, by narrowing his concerns and concentrating on his own job," Venturi wrote. His point was that the best way for an architect to fulfill his or her social responsibility is simply to build better buildings.

No one would deny that, but it is enough? Today, there is more public interest in new architecture than ever, and as we build museums, performing arts centers, academic buildings, and houses as one-of-a-kind, special monuments, it is easy to think of architecture only as an elaborately wrought physical object—as pure form—and not as a structure created to make a social statement of some kind. Architecture can, after all, provide a model for a way to live, or be a source of solutions to social problems. Karsten Harries, a contemporary philosopher with a particular interest in art and architecture, took some issue with the extent to which we, as a society, seem in thrall to eye-grabbing architecture in his book *The Ethical Function of Architecture,* which did not reject aesthetics so much as try to broaden the discussion. Architecture is too obsessed with form for its own sake, Harries argued. Architecture matters because it has responsibilities to society that are far broader than the making of even the most beautiful forms and shapes. To Harries, Nikolaus Pevsner's famous line about Lincoln Cathedral and the bicycle shed was wrong, not so much because it created a falsely simple distinction between architecture and building, but because its underlying rationale was limited to the way a building looked. Architecture, Harries wrote, "has to free itself from the aesthetic approach, which also means freeing itself from an understanding of the work of architecture as fundamentally just a decorated shed."

The aesthetic approach can also give architecture a hermetic quality, in which architecture becomes directed less to social needs than toward theoretical ideas and pure form. Architectural theory is capable of being a profound quest, but architecture is not, in the end, philosophical. There is always room for architecture that comments on other architecture and for architecture that is created mainly to promulgate an idea about architecture. But finally architecture is not about itself. As I said at the beginning of this chapter, it is about everything else. It is never a neutral envelope. It is always made to contain something, and to understand architecture fully you have to understand more than architecture. You have to understand something about what is going to be contained within a building, whether it is theater or medicine or high finance or baseball. You don't have to be able to conduct Mass to design a Catholic church or be able to direct *Hamlet* to design a theater, but if you have no interest whatsoever in the act of worship or the art of the theater, something important is likely to be lost. You don't need to be Derek Jeter to design a baseball park, but if you do not understand the game and know what it is like to sit for nine innings in what A. Bartlett Giamatti, the former Yale president turned baseball commissioner, once called "that simulacrum of a city . . . a green expanse, complete and coherent, shimmering," then you will not be able to design a baseball park as it should be. This is much more than a matter of providing commodity in the Vitruvian sense, much more than making sure that a building functions well on a practical level. Architecture exists to enable other things, and it is enriched by its intimate connection to those other things. To study school buildings is, in part, to study education; to study hospitals is, in part, to study medicine. The tie between architecture and the things it contains makes architecture different from anything else. Nothing else, you could say, is about everything.

Still, architecture is art, and as I will argue in the rest of this book, in the final analysis we cannot not view it through an aesthetic lens. But of course architecture also is not art. Karsten Harries proposed what he called the ethical approach to architecture in response to this paradox and as the alternative to the temptation to view architecture purely as aesthetics. An ethical approach to architecture, he said, should show us our place in the world and, Harries wrote, paraphrasing an idea put forth a generation earlier by Sigfried Giedion, "should speak to us of how we are to live in the contemporary world." Such architecture is invariably public, not private, and as such, it makes a statement about the importance of community; it is common ground, and it inspires us. "Architecture has an ethical function in that it calls us out of the everyday, recalls us to the values presiding over our lives as members of a society; it beckons us toward a better life, a bit closer to the ideal," Harries wrote. "One task of architecture is to preserve at least a piece of utopia, and inevitably such a piece leaves and should leave a sting, awaken utopian longings, fill us with dreams of another and better world."

I like Harries's notion of an ethical architecture, since it seems to say implicitly that even though architecture is an aesthetic experience, it is not in the same category as art and music. Rather, it is a way of providing something we absolutely need, and not a luxury that we can afford to give up in the face of stress and difficulty. Indeed, you could argue that an ethical architecture is more essential, not less essential, in times of difficulty, that it can rise to its greatest potential and be a symbol of what we want and what we aspire to, as so few other things can. It is not for nothing that Abraham Lincoln insisted that the building of the great dome of the Capitol continue during the Civil War, even though manpower was scarce and money scarcer still; he knew that the rising dome was a symbol of the nation coming together and that no words could have the same effect on the psyche of the country that the physical reality of this building could. Lincoln knew, I suspect, that even the most eloquent words would not be present and in front of us all the time, the way the building would be. And Lincoln knew also that there was value in making new symbols as well as in preserving older ones and that building the dome was a way of affirming a belief in the future.

It is hard to think of a more ethical approach to architecture than that. We build, in the end, because we believe in a future—nothing shows commitment to the future like architecture. And we build well because we believe in a better future, because we believe that there are few greater gifts we can give the generations that will follow us than great works of architecture, both as a symbol of our aspirations of community and as a symbol of our belief not only in the power of imagination but in the ability of society to continue to create anew. The case for architecture, if we are going to call it that, doesn't rest solely on the experience of being in remarkable and wonderful buildings—those places that, as Lewis Mumford once put it, "take your breath away with the experience of seeing form and space joyfully mastered." But those are the great moments of architecture, those moments that take the breath away, and they are the most important ones, the ones that make civilization. They are our cathedrals, both literally and figuratively, the works of architecture that add to our culture the way that works by Beethoven or Picasso add to our culture. To strive to make more of them is in its way an ethical as well as an aesthetic goal, because it is a sign that we believe our greatest places are still to be made and our greatest times are still to come.

2 challenge and comfort

I would rather sleep in the nave of Chartres Cathedral with the nearest john two blocks down the street than in a Harvard house with back-to-back bathrooms.

PHILIP JOHNSON

I n the previous chapter I spoke of how architecture is balanced between art and practicality, and how it can never be perceived as either art or utility but has to be both at once. Keeping a kind of "both/and" rather than "either/or" sense of architecture in one's head is an essential precondition to understanding. Still, it is the art that thrills as function never can; this is where passion arises and what makes architecture a transcendent experience. No one really remembers Chartres Cathedral because it housed thousands of the faithful efficiently, or Frank Lloyd Wright's Fallingwater because it gave the Kaufmann family of Pittsburgh a woodsy weekend retreat, or Thomas Jefferson's University of Virginia campus because it organized teachers and students in an effective way, though to be sure, each of these buildings did these things. We remember these works of architecture because they went beyond these mundane achievements, so far beyond as to become works of art capable of affecting vast numbers of people who were not part of these buildings' original communities of users at all. And they continue to affect people, just as powerfully—if not more so—than they did when they were new.

When architecture is art, it does not deny the ethical purpose proposed for it by Karsten Harries, with which I ended the last chapter. Indeed, it enhances it. What Harries calls the ethical function of architecture is necessary, and urgent, and transcends the gap between aesthetics and practical function. Chartres and the University of Virginia are both profoundly ethical buildings as well as great works of art. They are both buildings in which the aesthetic idea is deeply connected to a larger social idea and, indeed, is all but inseparable from it. We can approach these buildings as pure form if we wish, but we understand them far more deeply if we look at their aesthetics as connected to the social ideas the buildings represent—ideas which, in both of these cases, are communal and public and, in the case of Chartres, spiritual as well. I think we could also look at Fallingwater in terms of a social idea, the notion of family and nature, of home and hearth. It is not a public idea about community as in Chartres and the University of Virginia, but it is an ethical idea nonetheless.

When architecture is both beautiful and ethical, it invites belief. "It is not worth it to use marble for what you don't believe in, but it is worth it to use cinder blocks for that which you do believe in," said Louis Kahn, our age's truest architectural prophet, in a remark that both confirms the validity of architectural ambition and deflates pretension at the same time. Architecture as art emerges from a desire to do more than solve a functional problem. This deeper desire is itself, in a sense, its ethical function, a statement that the building's art exists not only for art's sake but also for the sake of some social purpose. Indeed, we might say that this is as good a definition of the ethical function as there could be—that when architecture is art, it is not art for art's sake but art for social purpose.

This is all the more true because much architecture that aspires to high art is not particularly beautiful by conventional measure. Kahn's work provides several vivid examples. Many of his buildings, such as his brick and concrete Unitarian Church of 1962 in Rochester, New York, where light washes the sanctuary as it tumbles down across raw concrete block, seem harsh at first; it is in their haunting quality that they achieve the sublime. The room is square, and natural light enters not through windows but indirectly through light towers that rise above the four corners of the space, so you do not see the source of the light but only experience it against the concrete block. The ceiling is of poured concrete, and with the corners open to the light towers, it appears to float over the middle of the space like a canopy. Kahn's Yale Art Gallery of 1953, also a building of brick with an interior largely of concrete, has a similar roughness, and as with the Unitarian Church its beauty does not emerge at first glance but comes only after time spent within it. The same might be said of his dormitory at Bryn Mawr College, Erdman Hall, a building of slate and concrete that deliberately eschews conventional symbols of domesticity. Kahn's buildings do not coddle us.

When architecture aspires to the seriousness of great art, it transcends both the banality of the homogeneous urban and suburban environment, now so drearily identical around the world, and the triviality of the theme park, that desperate cry for a sense of place. Christian Norberg-Schulz has written with great eloquence of the loss of sense of place in contemporary society, calling it "the loss of the poetic, imaginative understanding of the world," and argues for "a return to 'the things themselves.'" In

Louis Kahn, Unitarian Church, Rochester, New York

Architecture: Meaning and Place, he states that the alienation one feels in the contemporary physical environment is, in effect, the loss of aesthetic sensibility: "Life in fact does not consist of quantities and numbers, but of concrete things such as people, animals, flowers and trees, of stone, earth, wood and water, of towns, streets and houses, of sun, moon and stars, of clouds, of night and day and changing seasons. And we are here to care for these things."

Many of the architectural things we love best, and care for the most, are not of course works of art at all. Vernacular architecture, the unself-conscious, ordinary architecture of the everyday landscape, hovers over this book, I confess, like an old aunt, unsophisticated but with great natural wisdom, and deeply beloved for it. It is difficult not to cherish the tile-roofed, white houses of the Mediterranean, the shingled cottages of New England, the brick commercial buildings of the main streets of midwestern American cities. There is something in the way human beings are designed that reacts well to some shapes and not others, and these time-tested vernaculars reflect not only climatic and cultural conditions of their areas but also these inherently appealing shapes. Forget, for a moment, the vexing issue of McDonald's and the highway strip. What eye does not love a red-painted barn in a sloping meadow? It is both intrinsically attractive as a form and soothing as a symbol of a comfortable, ordered life. So, too, is it with a row of Italianate brownstones or a small Cape Cod cottage.

It is from the ordinary that we build perceptions and establish a foundation on which to appreciate and understand more ambitious forms of art. These things—architectural memories, we can call them—are the subject of chapter 5. Such buildings ground us. But they are folk melodies, not symphonies, and it is the point of this chapter to look more carefully at what we mean when we elevate architecture to the highest realm of art, and how the experience of looking at architecture as art differs from the experience of looking at buildings constructed in any vernacular, whether it is the nearly sublime vernacular of the New England barn or the more problematic architecture of the contemporary landscape of strip and sprawl.

It is no easier to say what makes a work of architecture succeed as art than to say what makes a great painting or great music. We are innately conservative; we are most comfortable with what we already know, and the omnipresence of vernacular building makes this even more the case with architecture than with literature or music. Yet every so often come innovations so powerful that they force their way through and make us see the world differently. These changes may be small; the notion that art, even great art, creates epiphanies is more the stuff of overblown memoirs than of real life. Rare is the life that is transformed by exposure to a single work of art. Yet art does change us, through exhilaration, shock, and a heightened sense of possibility. And once we have felt these, we are no longer the same.

Kahn, the greatest American architect since Frank Lloyd Wright, used to speak of great art not as the fulfillment of a need—"need is just so many bananas," he liked to say—but of the fulfillment of desire. Desire, not need, leads to great art, Kahn said—but when the artistic achievement is great enough, it becomes a new need. The world didn't need Beethoven's Fifth Symphony, Kahn said, until he wrote it. And after that, no one who ever heard it could conceive of living without it. We began to need Beethoven, not because of an innate need to do so, but because Beethoven's own desire, manifested in his art, made it so.

And as with the Fifth Symphony, the world was never again the same after Michelangelo's *David,* or *Hamlet,* or Picasso's *Les Demoiselles d'Avignon,* or *The Waste Land.* And so, too, with the Pyramids and Chartres Cathedral and Wright's Unity Temple and Le Corbusier's Villa Savoye and the Seagram Building by Mies van der Rohe and Kahn's own Salk Institute or a hundred other great buildings that have expanded our sense of human possibility.

Now, expanding a sense of human possibility is a lovely notion, but as a definition of great architecture it is vague and unsatisfying, and not only because there are disturbing as well as uplifting ways in which human possibility can be expanded—the discovery of germ warfare, for example, is not the same as the making of a work of art. Yet even left to its positive connotations, this phrase suggests a kind of well-meaning, New Age mission in which art provides a kind of warm bath, full of intellectual and spiritual uplift. Art—art of all kinds, not just architecture—exists to challenge, not to coddle. It often expands human possibility in ways that are hard to understand and are troubling, even shocking, to experience. Art, at its most important, is not merely a matter of looking at beautiful things. It can be difficult and disturbing. It forces us to see things differently, in part by breaking the mold of what has come before.

The new is often hard to accept; it can seem ugly or coarse. It is only seldom seen as beautiful. "I do not think of art as Consolation. I think of it as Creation. I think of it as an energetic space that begets energetic space," wrote Jeanette Winterson, who in another context observed, "The most conservative and least interested person will probably tell you that he or she likes Constable. But would our stalwart have liked Constable in 1824 when he exhibited at the Paris Salon and caused a riot? . . . To the average eye, now, Constable is a pretty landscape painter, not a revolutionary who daubed bright color against bright color ungraded by chiaroscuro. We have had 150 years to get used to the man who turned his back on the studio picture, took his easel outdoors and painted in the rapture of light. It is easy to copy Constable. It was not easy to be Constable."

Nor was it easy to be Joyce, or Stravinsky, or Juan Gris—or Le Corbusier or Mies van der Rohe or Louis Kahn or Robert Venturi or Frank Gehry or Rem Koolhaas or Zaha Hadid. In each case, artists have broken through convention and changed our notions of what a culture can produce. Their breakthroughs now please us and, if they remain as potent as they should, thrill us. Yet they were almost always initially unpopular and vastly misunderstood. And now it is not possible to imagine our culture without the things their passions made possible.

When architecture is art, it does not escape the obligation to be practical, and its practical shortcomings should not be forgiven. At least not entirely. Yet neither should practical matters play the dominant role in making judgments. It is churlish to complain that Frank Lloyd Wright's houses leak or that Le Corbusier's weather badly or that Frank Gehry's are difficult to construct, all of which may be more or less be true, but what of it? That leaky roof is not our problem, and neither is the fact that we might not wish to live in such a building ourselves. Le Corbusier's extraordinary Villa Savoye, completed in 1929 in Poissy, a suburban outside of Paris, was the subject of angry exchanges between the architect and Madame Savoye, who considered the house "uninhabitable," though she lived in it for more than a decade. Her discomfort is understandable, as was the anger felt

Le Corbusier, Villa Savoye, Poissy, France

toward Mies van der Rohe by Edith Farnsworth, who like the Savoyes commissioned one of the greatest houses of the twentieth century and, once living in it, found it woefully impractical.

The Savoyes and Edith Farnsworth were unlucky because they had to live with a work of art at every moment, a nearly impossible task. The rest of us have the luxury of looking at these houses only when we want to. Some people, of course, are capable only of looking at houses in practical terms. When Philip Johnson's Glass House, completed in 1949, was new, a pretentious woman who visited this then-shocking piece of modern architecture turned to its owner and said, "Very nice, but I couldn't live here."

Mies van der Rohe, Farnsworth House, Plano, Illinois

"I haven't asked you to, Madam," was Johnson's reply.

Exactly. And if we are lucky enough to be able to appreciate Building X or Building Y as a purely aesthetic experience, regardless of its usefulness, so much the better. Yes, the roof leaked in the Villa Savoye, but it didn't leak on you or me; and the glass walls of the Farnsworth House and its lack of screens did indeed make it exceedingly difficult to live in during the summer, but you and I were not trying to sleep there. As no man is a hero to his valet, few great houses are uplifting works of art to the people who live in them: these people are simply too close, and because they are there at every moment, they have no choice but to think of comfort. The rest of us can think of challenge, and of beauty, and treat them as works of genius, which are often incompatible with the demands of daily life. We enjoy the freedom of adventuring among masterpieces, to paraphrase Anatole France's definition of a critic's work, and keep in mind that the greatest joy of architecture is in the discovery of its ability to be art.

The point I am trying to make is that the notion of challenge that is so closely bound to the experience of art presents a particular dilemma so far as architecture is concerned, for architecture is necessarily ill at ease, if not incompatible, with it. If great art exists to challenge rather than coddle—or, in Jeanette Winterson's terms, as creation rather than as consolation—then what of architecture's obligation to provide shelter and comfort? Unlike art or literature, architecture must protect us from the elements, and it is omnipresent within our view. It must, in some way, console us, for its job is to protect us. We cannot live with architecture as constant challenge, any more than we can approach James Joyce as escape reading or treat John Cage as elevator music. Art demands attention, and architecture's constant presence in our lives makes constant attention to it impossible. This is actually true of every kind of architecture, from buildings that are designed only for comfort to the ones designed mainly to challenge us. Everyday architecture gives us some license to ignore it, to think of it as a kind of background hum, to be noticed only when it is exceptionally big, exceptionally ugly, or exceptionally beautiful. Most of the architecture that surrounds us we barely see; in architecture, familiarity often breeds not contempt but complacency.

The Savoyes and Edith Farnsworth would have been happy to settle for complacency, I suspect. It is no wonder that they were not happy. Even without leaky roofs and too much hot sun, it is difficult to live within a work of art every day of your life. The Savoyes and Edith Farnsworth chose their architects and approved their plans, of course, but that is beside the point; it merely adds a level of irony to their distress. Owners of houses by Frank Lloyd Wright speak of feeling Wright's presence at every moment, and they are not talking in spiritual or ghostly terms. They mean that every aspect of their houses is so powerfully shaped by Wright's aesthetic that they feel he is directing their movements and their feelings as they try to go about their daily lives. Most Wright owners are fiercely loyal to their houses, but it is not surprising that they seek a break from time to time from his relentless presence.

Architecture that has been designed to be a constant presence in our lives can also raise expectations far too high; even if it does not create the anguish felt by the Savoyes and Edith Farnsworth or force itself unceasingly on us like Wright's, it still seems to dangle before us a kind of ideal world, an aesthetic perfection that can all too easily be taken to feel like a salve for other wounds and a promise of perfection in other aspects of life. It is not, of course, so. Perfect architecture does not make our lives perfect. "The noblest architecture can sometimes do less for us than a siesta or an aspirin," the philosopher Alain de Botton wrote in *The Architecture of Happiness.* "Even if we could spend the rest of our lives in the Villa Rotunda or the Glass House, we would still often be in a bad mood."

The paradox of challenge and comfort goes to the core of architecture as art. If great art exists to challenge, and sometimes rejects the very possibility of comfort, can architecture, which must take such matters into account, ever be great art? Obviously it can be, and is. But art and comfort need not be a zero-sum game, however much Philip Johnson may have pretended so in the remark with which this chapter began. No one really lives in Chartres; no one expects a profound aesthetic experience from a Harvard dormitory. Take Johnson not literally but as a warning (he spoke these words in the early 1950s) against the mundane functionalism that dominated architectural culture in the postwar years. There is more to architecture than efficiency—there is art! Or so he was proclaiming.

It is worth pointing out here that of the buildings that disappoint, most do so not because of failure to deliver on their aesthetic aspirations but because their architects had given up on aesthetic aspirations altogether and thought only in terms of efficiency, and generally failed to deliver even that. It isn't the leaky-roofed masterwork that is the problem, in other words, it is the hospital that is a cold, forbidding environment to the patients who are there ostensibly to feel better and to the staff who work there every day; or it is the school that seems designed more for the ease of the custodial staff than for the pleasure of the students and teachers; or it is the airport with endless concourses that feel like overcrowded basements, laid out for the convenience of moving airplanes, not for the pleasure of people; or it is the strip mall that was designed solely to make it easier to drive cars in and out. Practicality and function are complicated things, if not quite as daunting as aesthetics, and when we talk about function, it is important to keep in mind just whose practicality and what function a building is intended to serve.

"Form follows function," that old chestnut of modern architecture, turns out, once you dig into it, to mean very little at all. There are just too many kinds of function, and too many ways different forms can serve the same function, for that line to be of any help at all. And is not visual pleasure, which that cliché willfully ignores, a kind of function, too?

It should be obvious by now that I much prefer the term "comfort," not because I think comfort is the same as practicality but because it seems to connect much more directly to the needs of people who actually use a building. A hospital may appear to be functioning well if it is laid out for efficient movement of patients to and from the operating room or the emergency room, but it may not be comfortable at all for those patients, and that is a far more important—we might even say a far more ethical— measure of what constitutes function. This is the essence of the idea behind a movement called "evidence-based design," which seeks to shift the architectural priorities in facilities such as hospitals to designs that have clearly been shown in research studies to improve patient health, as the design of a school should be driven by elements that make it pleasanter for students and teachers. The notion that scientific research might determine wise design directions is only beginning to take hold among both architects and the medical profession, but it is growing. The key elements of evidence-based design are simple and straightforward: greater connections to nature; a greater sense of choice so that patients can have more control over their environment; facilities to make it easy for spouses and others to be present to provide social support for patients; pleasant visual and aural distractions for patients; logical and comprehensible building layouts; and an avoidance of unpleasant or harsh noise, glaring light, or smells. Evidence-based design is intended not to devalue efficiency but to value serenity more.

The word "comfort" is also closer to contentment, and contentment is a worthy thing for architecture to inspire. I think it is what Alain de Botton (what is it about architecture that inspires philosophers to write books about it?) meant by the title of his book *The Architecture of Happiness,* in which he explored the connections between architecture, feeling, and human character, cautioning against believing that architecture could change lives by itself but celebrating its sway over our emotions nonetheless.

Comfort alone, or "contentment," if that term feels more natural to you, is enough some of the time, but not all of the time. What we need, more than anything, is to understand the importance of synthesis, which is to say the view that the unique thing about architecture is that it is within its rights to seek aesthetic challenge and physical comfort at the same time. That doesn't quite mean that a building should be expected to be difficult and to inspire contentment in equal measure—a near impossibility— but rather that these two qualities, which so rarely occur together, should be considered entitled to coexist. The synthesis required by architecture is far more subtle than that required by any other form of art. Every building contains tangible elements that respond to its practical aspects and intangible ones that respond to its aesthetic ambitions. "A great building," Kahn said, "must begin with the unmeasurable, go through measurable means when it is being designed, and in the end must be unmeasurable."

The answer to the architectural paradox is surely not to reject comfort altogether, as some architects have done, as if to say that aesthetic value comes in inverse proportion to the degree of contentment a building inspires. I think in particular of those architects who in the 1980s and 1990s identified with the Deconstructivist movement, proudly proclaiming the obligation of architecture to create a sense of dislocation and unease, ostensibly with the goal of reflecting the postmodern condition. (The work of architects such as Peter Eisenman in New York, Eric Owen Moss in Los Angeles, and the firm of Coop Himmelblau in Vienna, which depend heavily on colliding forms and sharp angles, provide examples of this.) This is architecture attempting to make an aesthetic statement that all but denies the responsibility of architecture to house human beings and to provide them with at least a modicum of comfort. This architecture of anxious angles and discordant forms avoids comfort as an end in itself and actively creates discomfort. This is not an architecture of synthesis but an architecture that comes from the idea that challenge is all that matters and rejects the idea of comfort as representing soft-headedness, even weakness. So, too, with buildings such as Minoru Yamasaki's Rainer Square skyscraper in

Seattle, which is balanced on a central concrete pier and looms ominously over the pedestrian, a simple and glib form of challenge that yields not profound experience but annoyance.

Yet the aim of such architecture is at least higher than that which goes to the other extreme and rejects challenge in favor of nothing but comfort: the revivalists who make Georgian villas and Spanish Colonial mansions, seeking an easy sentimentality. There has been a lot of architecture of this kind made in the current generation—more, probably, than at any other time since modernism began its rise into the mainstream in the 1920s. As I said in the previous chapter, much of it is of high quality. It offers all the consolation in the world, and given how much we need background buildings as well as foreground buildings (a subject I will discuss more fully in chapter 7), there is plenty of justification for it. But it abdicates the most serious ambitions of art and prefers the view that if architecture can provide a peaceful backdrop for a civilized life, it will have served its purpose.

Much of the time, perhaps even most of the time, that is true. The sprawling neo–Shingle Style houses of architects such as Robert A. M. Stern and Jaquelin Robertson, to name but two examples, are gracious and intelligently wrought homages to some of the greatest American architecture of all time. The models cannot be faulted, and neither can the execution. Such houses are easy to live in and beautiful to look at, and there is no question that they, like the best of the neo-Georgian, Spanish Colonial, and Neoclassical architecture produced today, achieve much of what architecture aspires to. They surely bring contentment, and often even joy. But if we desire masterpieces as well as civilized, comforting spaces, we must go beyond buildings like these, welcoming presences though they may be. They offer us not the difficult moments in which art moves forward but the easy moments in which art congratulates itself on what it has done. The Neoclassical house produced today is, to paraphrase Jeanette Winterson, Constable today, not Constable when new.

It is not the obligation of every building to push the art of architecture forward—and thank goodness for that, since it would make our cities cacophonies of ego—but it is essential to keep in mind that there is a difference between excellence that looks backward and excellence that strives to leap ahead and change the way people see the world. A sumptuous Georgian mansion on Long Island designed by Delano and Aldrich in the 1930s offers vast pleasures, and its qualities remain potent today—but it is Frank Lloyd Wright's Fallingwater that changed the world, and it is important not to forget the difference. Although the person who rejects the Georgian mansion as a stuffy remnant of a bygone era denies him or herself the opportunity to experience exquisitely wrought form, detail, and proportion, the person who considers Frank Gehry's Guggenheim Museum Bilbao just a chaotic assemblage of industrial elements has denied him- or herself something more profound, losing the chance to experience one of the late twentieth century's greatest and most thrilling works of art. Let architects reject one path or the other; connoisseurs of architecture must understand both the building that elevates comfort over challenge and the building that elevates challenge over comfort.

Can the two priorities of architecture as art—challenge and

comfort—be merged? Or, more to the point, can the two be merged without weakening both? We have already seen, in the Yamasaki skyscraper, how simpleminded challenge makes only for discomfort. Meeting halfway—through architecture that challenges a little and comforts a little but doesn't do quite enough of either—is a typical compromise, and the built world is full of them: look, for example, at so much late-twentieth-century corporate architecture, such as Kohn Pedersen Fox's sprawling, angular headquarters for the IBM Corporation in Armonk, New York, or that firm's super-tall skyscraper in Shanghai with a hole as its crown, which attempts to blend a sculptural statement with functional needs. But at its best, the synthesis architecture strives for is more profound than this and carries both challenge and comfort to a higher level.

Perhaps challenge is not the best term: perhaps intensity of feeling is. That, surely, is the reason that the Gothic buildings at Yale by James Gamble Rogers are so successful, despite their somewhat soft intellectual underpinnings. They are not only stunningly beautiful, they connect with a laserlike directness to an institution's sense of itself, and if that sense is lacking in the ironic edge that we have come to expect of architecture at the end of the twentieth century, no matter. In structures like Rogers's Harkness Tower, the climactic element of his Memorial Quadrangle (now Branford and Saybrook Colleges), or his Berkeley and Trumbull and Jonathan Edwards Colleges, innocence rises to a kind of heroic grandeur, and it has a very different quality from the self-indulgence that characterizes so much other purely historicist architecture. The historical replication in these Yale buildings isn't like that of the pseudo-Mediterranean villas put up by real estate developers; these are truly heroic statements. Like the Woolworth Building or Grand Central Terminal or the New York Public Library, the Yale buildings bespeak a potent civic presence, not to mention a visual magnificence, that transcends the absence of what we have called challenge. And these buildings (which I use here to stand for many other great works that rely on the architecture of the past) are also deeply ethical, to return again to that aspect of the architectural equation. In many ways, it is what Karsten Harries has called the ethical function that brings challenge and comfort together: the building whose high aesthetic ambitions exist also to fulfill a social purpose. When a building succeeds at its high aesthetic ambitions and possesses a meaningful and convincing social purpose, it works on a level that relatively few structures do. And in its ethical function, it challenges us even if its architects may have intended mainly to comfort us.

The greatest architecture inspires awe. It stuns us, and it stops us in our tracks. It leaves us speechless. In the making of special, intense, poetically crafted space—"ineffable space," as Le Corbusier called it, for great architectural space, like great music and poetry, can never be described adequately—is where the architect's highest aesthetic achievement comes. Space (which is discussed more fully in chapter 4) is architecture's aesthetic reality, at least as much as the walls and floors and the details and ornaments that surround it.

If the most exquisitely made space is capable of evoking feelings of awe, this is not to diminish the importance of the mass

James Gamble Rogers, Harkness Tower, Yale University, New Haven

and shape of a building's exterior. Great works are always compositions, combinations of solids and voids and horizontals and verticals put together as we had never imagined possible, to make the same stunning response as the space itself. Not for nothing did Vitruvius select the word "delight" as the third portion of his tripartite definition of architecture; great architecture must evoke indescribable joy.

Joy and challenge? How can these two things go together? How can there be joy in great architecture if its mission is to challenge, to upset the order of the universe as we know it? It would seem as if joy should go with complacency, not with challenge; by logic the joy ought to belong to the hesitant, unchallenging, but thoroughly comfortable neo-Georgian mansion, not to the daring object that resembles nothing we have ever seen before. Yet this is the magic of architecture's synthesis: when it works right, as in the masterworks of every age including our own, it startles us and comforts us at the same time. There is something serene about most great architecture, even as it surprises us. Even the deliberate distortions of classical form by the Italian Mannerists, from Michelangelo to Giulio Romano; the extraordinary classical virtuosity of Nicholas Hawksmoor or Sir John Soane or Sir Edwin Lutyens; the laser-like intensity of Le Corbusier; the aloof coolness of Mies van der Rohe; the passionate, almost mystical forms of Louis Kahn; the contemporary mannerism of Robert Venturi; the seemingly disordered forms of Frank Gehry —all of these can shock, and often do, particularly those who see them for the first time. Yet in other ways they are deeply reassuring, for they create space and form that communicate their essence to us powerfully, and warmly. They seek to delight the eye in new ways but do not reject the notion of delight any more than they reject the other aspects of the Vitruvian equation. They interpret delight as emotional intensity, which is something that great architecture has always been able to inspire. A great building must have a use, it must stand up—and it must be a work of art.

3
architecture

as object

Architecture is the play of forms—
wise, correct, magnificent—the play
of forms in the light.

LE CORBUSIER

The sun never knew how great it
was until it hit the side of a
building.

LOUIS KAHN

A rchitecture is physical form. However much we consider its cultural meanings, its symbolism, its social value, or how the computer-driven world of cyberspace is creating new concepts of virtual space, the reality of architecture remains: buildings, not concepts, and how buildings combine to make places that are larger than their parts. Architecture is built form in the physical world and must be understood, experienced, and judged by the standards of built form in the physical world. The traditional principles still apply: architecture depends for its effectiveness on the extent to which the portions of a structure relate to one another and to the whole, and also how they relate to the human form. Every building connects to the way the eye perceives both space and composition. Whatever else may contribute to the way we experience it—the way it relates to memory, the extent to which it functions smoothly or not, the degree of physical comfort it offers—our relationship to a building almost always begins with the way it looks.

This remains true despite the overwhelming effect that the computer, the enabler of the virtual world, has had on the process of design and construction. Even though all kinds of buildings, from Frank Gehry's extraordinary sculptural shapes like the Guggenheim Museum Bilbao and the Walt Disney Concert Hall in Los Angeles to the latest generation of super-tall skyscrapers like the Burj Dubai, could not have been built without the aid of computer-driven technologies, and digital technology now makes it possible to create more effective representation of real space than ever before, the basic truth does not change: architecture is buildings, and buildings have a physical reality. They have tops, bottoms, and sides. They have facades, or fronts, which are both visual compositions and public faces. They have interiors, which are both to be used as rooms and felt as three-dimensional space. They have overall form and shape, which can be seen from afar and from up close, and which may appear altogether different depending on your vantage point. The physical reality of buildings, both great and ordinary, obliges us to think of them, first and foremost, as objects.

In *Round Buildings, Square Buildings, and Buildings That Wiggle Like a Fish,* by Philip M. Isaacson, a lyrical paean to the joy of architecture written for children, there are chapters titled "Thick Walls and Thin Walls," "Light and Color," "Old Bones and New Bones" (about frameworks), and "Indoor Skies" (about ceilings). There are no chapters about how buildings function or why they are built or how they get constructed, not because Isaacson thinks that these things don't matter but because he knows that they are not the best way in, so to speak. Similarly, in his excellent but rather more turgid book *Experiencing Architecture,* Steen Eiler Rasmussen has given chapters names like "Solids and Cavities in Architecture," "Rhythm and Architecture," "Scale and Proportion," and "Architecture Experienced as Color Planes"— less lilting phrases, but the point is the same. You cannot love architecture without caring about how buildings look, and taking pleasure in that. If you do not respond to the physical appearance of buildings—if, say, when you are looking at a white clapboard church on a New England green, you can't come to sense the exuberance of the way its steeple meets the sky, or the welcoming grandeur of its front door, or the crisp, flat feeling of its walls—then you will never understand architecture, no matter how much you know about the reasons buildings come to be or the process of constructing them.

Of course the physical reality of buildings is only a part of the story. Buildings are public presences, and even as we evaluate them as physical form, it is vital to remember that every building also has a social and political, as well as a financial, reality and that we ignore these other dimensions of architecture at our peril. Indeed, proper respect for at least the social and political sphere is essential to understanding architecture. Who could judge a work of public housing purely as an aesthetic object, apart from the lives of the people within it? Or a hospital separate from the degree to which it facilitates caring for the sick? Or a military compound without any thought to the purposes for which was made?

None of these things are objects alone. They are structures that make social statements within a sociopolitical realm. They are statements of society's values. So, too, with a concert hall or a library or a museum or a shopping mall, each of which represents a commitment of resources, and our view of that commitment must affect our opinion of the building that it brings forth. Would we think of Albert Speer's vision for Berlin differently had it not been designed for the Nazi regime? (I suspect not, since the overbearing grandiosity and banality that makes it so difficult for us to accept Speer aesthetically is precisely what attracted his Nazi clients to his work.) Perhaps more to the point, do we allow our view of anyone who builds—whether it is a museum board risking its financial security on a daring new structure by a young architect or a school district insisting that it wants to build only plain-vanilla architecture or a hedge-fund manager showing off his wherewithal by erecting a pretentious mock-French château —to color our aesthetic judgment? It is impossible not to, at least to some extent. But yet another of the challenges of understanding architecture is to know when it is appropriate to allow social issues to play a major role in judgment and when it makes more sense to keep them in the background. If we were to reject all architecture produced by and for countries with whose policies we do not agree—or even by and for people with whom we do not agree—we would be rendering the whole notion of architectural judgment ridiculous by making aesthetics altogether irrelevant. Yet we cannot pretend that any building exists in an aesthetic vacuum, apart from any other concerns.

For the next few pages, though, I ask you to put aside these other concerns and think only in terms of what a building looks like when you stand before it. This task is difficult enough, given that there really is no single way of analyzing buildings or even a common set of criteria by which to judge their aesthetics. Even within the realm of visual perception, there is no clear set of priorities. What do you look at first? Does a building's facade matter the most in determining whether it is an aesthetic success?

Or is it a question of how all its sides come together to create a coherent object? Or is neither of these things as important as the nature and quality of the space within? And if it is the facade that you look at first, is it a matter of how well crafted it is as an artistic composition? Or do you wonder how appropriate and how physically appealing the materials are? What if the composition feels right but the colors seem wrong? Or if the color is right but the ornament and decoration feel off? Is the facade too busy, too spare, too fussy, or too austere? If it is a building that has been designed in some traditional style, is it to be judged by its degree of faithfulness to that style? And if it has been designed to be new and different, is it to be judged by the extent to which it is unlike anything else you have seen before?

Complex questions all, and none of them can be taken entirely on its own. They connect to one another, and perhaps the most important thing to say at this point is that some things matter more in certain situations and other things matter more in others. We are lucky that there is no way to rank buildings on some sort of absolute aesthetic scale—or perhaps it is better to say that it is just as well that attempts to quantify aesthetics have always failed, first because they ignore the fact that art, at its best, involves an instinctive sense that a kind of magic is being performed, a magic that, by its very nature, we cannot deconstruct and reconstruct as a formula to be used by others; and second, more specific to architecture than other arts, because turning aesthetics into numbers does not take into account the myriad of circumstances that form the context for the understanding of any building. And by context I mean not only the physical context—whether it is an urban building on a narrow street, a tower beside a freeway, a building in rolling farmland or in deep forest or on a suburban cul-de-sac—but also the temporal context, the time in which it was built, and often enough the political context, too, within which the architect has had to operate. And then, as I said above, there are the intentions of the designers and builders, and the building's uses, and so forth. Every one of these things can have some impact on aesthetics. But how we determine how much each of them matters, if it matters at all, is itself part of the challenge.

And then, when you have fully digested the object, so to speak, there is the question of how it connects to other buildings —how well the object relates to the other objects around it. In the end, architecture is an art of specifics, not of generalities, which is why it is more fruitful by far to try to grasp some of these ideas not by looking for formulas but by talking about the look and feel of actual buildings.

Let me begin by saying something about an American monument almost everyone knows, the Lincoln Memorial, and how it relates to the great Greek temple on which it was loosely based, the Parthenon: a pair of buildings that represent a similar aesthetic but which are notably, even overwhelmingly, different. The Lincoln Memorial, that marble box wrapped in thirty-six columns that sits at the end of the Mall in Washington, is obviously a Greek temple in one sense, and in another it is not a Greek temple at all. The architect Henry Bacon created a masterwork that in many ways is as inventive and original as the modernist buildings created in Europe at the same time—1915–22—as the memorial was designed.

Bacon used the vocabulary of Greek architecture (actually, Greco-Roman architecture, since it possesses the shared characteristics of both of these classical styles), but he used it brilliantly to his own purpose, which was to create an immense, formal box to memorialize Abraham Lincoln and stand as a symbol of American certitude and conviction. The memorial closes off the vista that begins with the United States Capitol two miles to the east, and it sits at the end of a reflecting pool, from a distance appearing, like the Taj Mahal, almost to float on the water. This is one of the great scenographic buildings of all time, and if it is not sensual enough by day, look at it at night, when the soft lighting makes the marble box glow behind the Doric columns, which appear dark behind the white marble, jumping out visually like the image in a photographic negative.

Bacon started with the Parthenon, yet he all but turned it inside out. The Lincoln Memorial is not a structure supported by columns, like a Greek temple, but more of a marble box surrounded by a colonnade. The walls are set inside, behind the columns, and they shoot straight up beyond them. The effect— again, slightly more dramatic with night lighting—is of a classical coating applied to a brooding, almost primal geometric form. There is no attempt, then, to mimic the appearance of a real Greek temple; it is hard not to think that Bacon's real interest was to communicate the power of abstract form and the strength of silence.

Henry Bacon, Lincoln Memorial, Washington, D.C.

Steen Eiler Rasmussen has written that architectural perception is intimately connected with feels of hardness and softness, heaviness and lightness, solid and void, a kind of visual dialectic or rhythm. The Lincoln Memorial demonstrates all of this clearly: the hardness of the sharply defined form plays off against the (relative) softness of Daniel Chester French's statue of a seated Lincoln; we could say that the heaviness of the boxy structure is lightened by the columns, and the columns and the space behind them surely represent the dialectic between solid and void. Rasmussen believed that these visual rhythms are universal, however differently they might be expressed in different kinds of buildings. "Most buildings consist of a combination of hard and soft, taut and slack, and of many kinds of surfaces," he wrote in *Experiencing Architecture.* "These are all elements of architecture, some of the things the architect can call into play. And to experience architecture, you must be aware of all of these elements."

But there is more to say about the Lincoln Memorial that goes beyond Rasmussen's criteria. To better balance the Capitol at the other end of the Mall, Bacon rotated his temple so that the long side served as the main facade and entrance, not the short end as at the Parthenon. He also eliminated the gabled attic present in real Greek temples ("attic" means Greek top), replacing it with a flat roof, rendering the building all the more abstract. If the Lincoln Memorial does nothing else, it can stand as a reminder that the mere presence of elements from classical architecture does not mean much when analyzing a building. The vocabulary of historical style can be used much more creatively than pure replication. In this case Bacon combined urbanistic concerns with scenographic ones to yield a building of startling grandeur and self-assurance.

Still, to most people the Lincoln Memorial is remembered as a bigger, grander, and more pompous Parthenon. Is this vast, white, hard marble building too cold, too austere, to stand as a proper memorial to Lincoln, a man of few pretensions? It is hard to disagree with Lewis Mumford, who asked, "Who lives in that shrine—Lincoln, or the men who conceived it?" But the men who conceived it did understand how to make architecture majestic, and that is their greatest triumph and ultimately the noblest tribute to Lincoln that can be imagined. Henry Bacon saw how to make Greek architecture an American cathedral.

Most writers who have tried to analyze the experience of look-ing at buildings have, like Rasmussen, dealt primarily with visual perception and said relatively little about symbolism, and often surprisingly little about style. William Caudill, William Peña, and Paul Kennon in *Architecture and You* suggest three ways of perceiving shapes: as plastic, or shaped and molded; as planar, or made up mainly of intersecting planes or surfaces; and as skele-tal, or seen primarily as a frame, with a sense that space moves through it. Eero Saarinen's TWA Terminal at John F. Kennedy Airport in New York is a prime example of a plastic building, as is a Frank Gehry building like the Walt Disney Concert Hall in Los Angeles. Mies van der Rohe's Barcelona Pavilion of 1929 surely illustrates the second type, and Le Corbusier's Unité d'Habita-tion, in Marseilles, of 1953, with its powerful concrete grid, is a well-known work of the third type. This distinction is useful, so far as it goes, but like all formulas it prefers neatness of categori-zation to reality, and ignores the fact that most architecture does not fit precisely into these types of form—while many buildings combine all three.

These categories will mean little if you are trying to under-stand your house, and they are of scant help, say, in analyzing skyscrapers. Rasmussen's observations, while hard to argue with, don't take us too far with tall buildings, either. If you look at three of the most important postwar American skyscrapers—Mies van der Rohe's great Seagram Building on Park Avenue in New York, Edward Durell Stone's General Motors Building on Fifth Avenue in New York, and I. M. Pei and Henry Cobb's John Hancock Tower on Copley Square in Boston—you can see that other ways of looking are needed. Too many other factors come into play. The darkly elegant Seagram Building presents a reserved, symmetrical rectangle to the street, and it rises behind an expansive, open plaza. To approach it across the plaza creates a sense of occasion; you feel almost compelled to walk in a straight line toward the entrance rather than to amble casually across it. The much taller, glaringly white General Motors Building is also symmetrical and set back from the street, but for years it made a ceremonial, stately approach like the one to the Seagram Building impossible, since the G.M. Building had a sunken plaza, and to reach the front door you had to walk around what amounted to a huge hole, a full level deep, at the edge of Fifth Avenue. (Now the plaza has been filled in and turned into a below-ground Apple Computer store, its entry an exquisite and enticing glass box that makes a splendid focal point for a vastly improved plaza that is where plazas ought to be, at street level.) As for the Hancock Tower, there is barely an entrance at all. This tower has an unusual shape, a slab sliced on the diagonal so that from some angles it appears like a thin wafer and from others, almost like a flat surface with nothing behind it at all. It is like a piece of abstract sculpture, beautiful but mute, and any door would appear to violate its perfection. No wonder the architects decided to tuck a discreet door onto the ground floor; they wanted us to barely notice it. The idea here is to minimize procession and to think of the building as an elegant, sculptural object set within the complex composition of Copley Square.

The surface structure of the Seagram Building is made of bronze, giving it a deep brown hue. In between the windows,

Mies van der Rohe and Philip Johnson, Seagram Building, New York

metal beams, called I-beams, rise all the way up the facade, a kind of modernist form of decoration. They give the facade depth and texture, just as traditional moldings do, and they create a rhythm for the eye. The General Motors Building is sheathed in white marble, and it, too, has vertical lines running all the way up, but instead of the delicate and understated texture of Mies's I-beams, these vertical lines are thick white stripes. The windows, instead of being flat, are all three-part bay windows, so the facade has a kind of rhythm, but it is more of an undulation. The Hancock Tower is light in color like the General Motors Building, but in every other way it could not be more different: it is sheathed in reflective glass, and the surface of its facade is absolutely flat; it appears to have no depth. There is deliberately no texture to it, and no ornament; only the shape itself, and the grid pattern of the flat, reflective windows, engage the eye.

Those windows began to fall out when the building was nearly finished, in the mid-1970s; after extended litigation they were replaced by similar-looking panels of different construction, but for an extended period the building was sheathed not in glass but in plywood and was known less as a major work of architecture than as the site of one of the most embarrassing construction errors of all time.

Once the new glass was put in, you could finally see that Hancock was designed to look as if it had been conceived as a pure abstraction, a cool, elegant piece of modern sculpture. It appears almost weightless, despite its size. Seagram, by contrast, seems to have the weight, the bearing, and the formality of a traditional building. It may have been designed by one of the twentieth century's great masters of modern architecture, but it seems intent on respecting architectural conventions, not over-turning them. The proportions of its windows are elegant, and you sense that behind each pane is life and activity—indeed, you can often see it. At the General Motors Building, Edward Durell Stone seems to have tried even harder than Mies van der Rohe to respect architectural conventions, but he has done it with a much heavier hand. The bay window, a staple of small houses, seems oddly out of place when it is replicated by the hundreds, and the rhythms and textures of this facade are clunky more than graceful. As for the Hancock building, Pei and Cobb's very point was to push the envelope of architectural convention. Hancock's panes of glass look like panels, not actual windows, and because they are all mirrors, you can see nothing behind them. But you can see neighboring buildings like Henry Hobson Richardson's great Trinity Church reflected in them, not to mention the blue or the gray of the Boston skies.

When you look at the Seagram Building or the General Motors Building or the Hancock Tower, you see not only an object but also a certain vision of the world. Architecture, among other things, seeks to establish order. Mies's order is easy to see—subtle and understated, but powerful and self-assured. The Seagram Building is far from small, but its scale is not overwhelming; indeed, the building seems to have been designed with a sense of human size always in mind. Its design appears simple at first glance, but the extraordinary precision of its detail and the serenity of its proportions are anything but casual. If the Seagram Building has a Zen simplicity to it, the General Motors Building suggests a more garish view of the world, one in which a few eye-grabbing gestures, like the white marble and the bay windows, are expected to create an aesthetic experience and to hide the fact that the building is, at the end of the day, a dressed-up box. Mies does not try to hide the fact that he has designed a box, and instead helps us find a tranquil and deep beauty in it; Stone seems to believe that there can be no true beauty in such simplicity and wants to fancy everything up.

Edward Durell Stone, General Motors Building, New York

The vision Pei and Cobb suggest with the Hancock Tower is a more difficult and complex one—full of movement and lines of tension. They did not want to compete head-on with Mies van der Rohe in the category of boxlike high-rises, and they chose to make their skyscraper in another shape altogether, a shape that in its very sleekness suggests that it is pushing the art of sky-scraper design forward. (The Seagram Building went up in the late 1950s, the General Motors Building in the 1960s, and the

I. M. Pei and Partners, John Hancock Tower, Boston

Hancock Tower in the 1970s, and while neither of the later two buildings was designed in direct response to its predecessor, it is hard not to think that their architects wanted to do something different from what had come before.) The General Motors Building has little to do with its surroundings, an indifference that its original, little-mourned sunken plaza made far worse than it is today, while the Seagram Building, despite being a structure of glass on a street that, at least in the 1950s, was made entirely of masonry buildings, was carefully aligned on a symmetrical axis opposite its classical neighbor, the Racquet and Tennis Club by McKim, Mead and White across Park Avenue. When you stand in front of the Seagram Building, you can feel an imaginary line that runs right through the center of its facade, across the plaza, across the street, and then right into the center of the Racquet Club. As for the Hancock Tower, paradoxically, even though its reflective glass would appear to signify the ultimate diffidence and aloofness—you can't see in, and there is no sign of human activity from the outside—the reflected images of surrounding buildings, not to mention the general sense of energy of its crisp shape, make you feel a connection between the tower and its urban surroundings. This building feels right for its place, almost in spite of itself.

"Form is a mystery which eludes definition but which makes man feel good in a way quite unlike social aid," Alvar Aalto, the great Finnish architect, said in a lecture in 1955. He was right. But while we will never fully understand why form—by which Aalto meant anything having to do with the way we perceive the physical presence of a building, be it the facade, the overall shape, the ornament, or the spaces within—can instill an emotional response, we cannot leave it at that. We can admit that there is no complete answer, but there are partial answers to why your eye takes pleasure in some forms and displeasure in others.

Stanley Abercrombie, in *Architecture as Art,* an introduction to architecture from the standpoint of aesthetic analysis, argues that shapes—basic geometric shapes—have a wholeness and a com-

Exterior view, Pantheon, Rome

pleteness that is inherently compelling. "Shapes arrest our attention, invite our curiosity, thrill us or repel us in the greatest possible variety of ways," Abercrombie writes. "Some, because they come laden with specific messages, affect us in ways that are easily understood, others in ways difficult to explain. With or without explanation, the power of shapes is indisputable."

Surely this is one of the reasons that the Pantheon in Rome is such an extraordinary building: a cylinder topped by a low dome with a Corinthian portico in front, it is actually a combination of simple shapes, but the cylinder is what holds your attention, even with the immense colonnade of the portico. The Pantheon is a composition of circles: the interior space is circular, the interior of the dome is a half-sphere, the open oculus at the top of the dome is another circle, and of course the columns, although they support a rectangular portico, are circles as well. The proportions of the Pantheon enhance the sense of pure and simple geometry: the diameter of the circle is 142 feet, and the height to the top of the dome is exactly the same. If the half-sphere of the dome were given a bottom half to create a complete sphere, it would fit perfectly inside the building; by the same token, the entire building could fit perfectly into an imaginary cube.

Pyramids, whether the vast, great Pyramids of Egypt or I. M. Pei's glass pyramid at the Louvre in Paris, or even a tiny pyramidal paperweight, exude a sense of strength. Nothing, after all, can knock over a pyramid. If nothing else, it is stable. But it is also easy to identify and easy to understand. There is no mystery to a pyramid, at least as a pure geometric form. But for almost everyone the pyramid has the added advantage of a deep well of associations. A pyramid *is* Egypt, if you want it to be, and even if you do not share the ancient Egyptians' belief that the gilt-covered point at the top could make manifest the sun god Ra as it reflected the morning sun, you cannot fail to feel that all pyramids somehow connect you to ancient civilization.

I. M. Pei quite ingeniously took advantage of these associations when he designed the glass pyramid that was constructed in 1989 to serve as a new entrance, and effectively a new symbol, for the Louvre in Paris. A structure of glass and steel in the middle of the courtyard of the Louvre seemed, at first, like the least appropriate thing imaginable. It was not only introducing modernity to a sixteenth-century space, it was bringing a quality of sleekness and an aesthetic that we might associate more with industrial design than with a former royal palace in France. But Pei defended his design on the basis of the ancient lineage of the

I. M. Pei, glass pyramid, Louvre Museum, Paris

pyramid. It was, he argued, not a modern shape at all but one of the oldest and most basic shapes in architecture; he was only building it out of modern materials. Pei turned out to be right. The glass pyramid and the old wings of the Louvre that surround it coexist with a remarkable degree of ease. The pyramid creates an elegant punctuation mark in the middle of the courtyard; the rest of the Louvre provides a perfect backdrop for the light, airy presence of the pyramid.

Not the least of the reasons the Louvre pyramid turned out to be successful is that, to return to Steen Eiler Rasmussen's ways of looking at things, it represents lightness amid heaviness, and transparency amid solidity. The pyramid works well also because of its size, which is big enough to hold its own in the large courtyard and serve as a fitting entrance to the vast museum, yet

Veldon Simpson, Luxor Hotel, Las Vegas

small enough not to overpower the older buildings. And the precision of Pei's detailing helps as well, by making clear that the pyramid, for all its stylistic difference from the rest of the Louvre, represents continuity in the sense that it, too, is an exquisitely wrought, one-of-a-kind object, the farthest thing in the world from a mass-produced, contemporary commercial building.

You could not say that about the Luxor Hotel in Las Vegas, designed by Veldon Simpson, which also has a glass pyramid, executed with none of Pei's finesse. The Luxor pyramid, which encloses a set of fairly conventional hotel rooms around an open atrium, is sheathed in a nondescript, brown-tinted reflective glass, making the building indistinguishable from a commercial office building but for its shape. The space in the center of the Luxor is awkwardly laid out; the clarity that the pyramid promises from outside is not delivered within. The fact is that pyramids are not particularly practical forms for most building functions, which is why there are few of them around that are not monuments of some kind. Pei's pyramid at the Louvre is only an entry pavilion leading to an underground lobby, and so it had few real functions. It could be open and transparent, a pure, abstract shape in glass like the Apple cube in front of the General Motors Building, also an entry pavilion. But at the Luxor in Las Vegas, the notion of the design was to create a casino hotel with an Egyptian theme, and the architects had to accommodate all kinds of conventional functions, many of which they couldn't fit at all and had to relegate to adjacent, boxy wings. The pyramid was used as an iconic symbol and as a container for a portion of the hotel's rooms and public spaces, but the constraints of its shape were such that it would have been impossible to put the entire hotel and casino into it unless it were to be built at a size so gargantuan as to make no sense, since most of the space in the middle would have gone to waste.

Simple shapes can be a Procrustean bed for architecture. So it was at the Luxor, and it was also the case at the Hirshhorn Museum on the Mall in Washington, designed by Gordon Bunshaft of Skidmore, Owings and Merrill and completed in 1974. Bunshaft clearly wanted a museum that didn't look like other museums, or much like anything else, for that matter, and he came up with a cylindrical building with a round court in the middle, a shape that relates in no clear way either to its function as a museum or to the forms and shapes of the buildings around it. It is little more than a concrete donut, a round bunker that signifies nothing about art and nothing about the civic role that

Skidmore, Owings and Merrill, Hirshhorn Museum, Washington, D.C.

any public museum must play. The donut form yields internal galleries that are round, but they have none of the spatial pleasures of Wright's Guggenheim in New York; these are merely confusing and awkward. The Hirshhorn is a geometric form disconnected from its function and from its surroundings, a chunky flying saucer on the Mall. Here, an architect seems to have abandoned convention in favor of what can only be called an obsession with geometries, a determination to play with abstract shapes to the exclusion of common sense. If the Hirshhorn were beautiful we might forgive its arrogance and indifference to both tradition and function—breathtaking beauty can allow you to get away with a lot in architecture, as in life. But after more than a generation, which is generally long enough for the cycles of taste to come around, this form looks as heavy and graceless as it did when it was brand-new.

The Rose Center for Earth and Space at the American Museum of Natural History in New York, designed by the Polshek Partnership and completed in 2000, uses an even more basic shape, a sphere, to somewhat better advantage, but not without major practical compromises as well. Do they matter? Less, I think, because Polshek's sphere, unlike Bunshaft's donut, seems serene and less forced. The center contains the museum's planetarium, which Polshek placed in an immense sphere, which itself is set within a four-story-high glass box. The sphere was inspired by one of the most famous unbuilt designs in the history of architecture, Étienne-Louis Boullée's proposal in 1784 for a spherical monument to Isaac Newton that would have been punctured by tiny holes to create the illusion of stars—in effect, an early planetarium. Spheres, like pyramids, have a powerful visual impact, but they do not lend themselves easily to some of the more conventional demands of architecture. How do you support it? And where do you put the door? Boullée set his sphere into a huge base and cut a tiny arch in the bottom; Polshek anchored his on gigantic legs, giving it something of the appearance of a vast piece of machinery, not quite consistent with the image of pure and perfect geometrical form. He put a door in the in the middle, along the equator, so to speak, with bridges connecting it to side balconies containing stairs and elevators. The most elegant solution to the impossible problem of putting a door in a sphere is the one used by Wallace K. Harrison for the Perisphere, the spherical symbol of the 1939 New York World's Fair: an escalator climbing up to an entry door in the middle, and then a swirling exit ramp that circled down the side of the sphere.

Polshek Partnership, Rose Center, American Museum of
Natural History, New York

If a sphere inside a glass box doesn't make for the easiest or
most logical entrance, it makes up for the awkwardness of moving into, around, and through it by its sheer presence. The Rose
Center is the kind of building that leads you to be forgiving of
functional compromises, since the beauty of that huge sphere
surrounded by its glass enclosure, sitting within a park-like setting on the north side of the museum, is like nothing else in New
York, or anywhere: an abstraction turned into a scientific exhibition, making real Boullée's eighteenth-century fantasy with

twenty-first-century technology. At night it is bathed in a soft, blue light, and it takes on an ethereal quality that makes it seem even less like a conventional building, and more alluring still.

The fewer functional demands, the more likely it is that a piece of architecture that is based on a simple geometric shape will work. Robert Mills's design for the Washington Monument, a 555-foot-tall obelisk, is the perfect example: it has no function at all, except to be there, the one structure in the District of Columbia that is permitted to rise higher than the dome of the Capitol. Yes, you can go up to the top of the monument and look out a tiny window, but that is quite beside the point, which is really just to look at it from afar, to feel its clarity and simplicity and directness and, if you wish, to let those characteristics of the obelisk remind you of similar traits in George Washington. The monument invokes both Washington's singularity and a sense of connection to ancient times and, by implication, to all of history. We are lucky, by the way, that Mills's original plan to surround the base of the obelisk with a classical colonnade was never realized—it would only have compromised the strength and directness of the monument as it now exists, a truly pure shape.

Pure geometric shapes had a particular attraction for modern architects in the early decades of the twentieth century, as they struggled to break free of what, to them, was the fussy and deadening clutter of nineteenth-century architecture. Thus Le Corbusier celebrated the factories and the grain elevators of the American Midwest, which he found far more appealing than almost anything else being erected in the United States. To architects who were trying to express "honesty" in construction

—and let us leave aside for the moment the question of just what honesty actually is in architecture, or if there even is such a thing—a grain elevator in particular seemed like a perfect marriage of form and function. It had no excess, no frilly decorations, nothing contorted for formal effect: just high, big, round cylinders, joined together to create a form that, whatever its mundane purpose, seemed to have a monumental presence. Le Corbusier called American grain elevators "the magnificent first fruits of the new age."

A reminder that the allure of simple, or relatively simple, geometric shapes has not disappeared: the 30 St. Mary Axe tower in London by Norman Foster, popularly known as "the gherkin," and the nearly-as-pickle-shaped Agbar Tower in Barcelona by Jean Nouvel, both skyscrapers of the twenty-first century. Foster's tower widens slightly as it rises, then tapers toward its rounded top; Nouvel's starts out as an ellipse in plan, with its walls straight up and down, then tapers toward a similarly rounded top. The phallic aspect of skyscrapers is an old story, but whatever else can be said about the shape of these buildings, they may be remembered best for how they have given that familiar metaphor a new lease on life, offset somewhat, perhaps, by the fact that both buildings are sheathed entirely in that least anthropomorphic of materials, glass. Foster's glass is set in a spiral pattern that seems intended to emphasize the tower's geometry. The Nouvel building's glass skin is more high-tech—it has a complex layer of casements that adjust to create a constantly changing pattern intended to resemble fluid: the simple geometric shape turned into expressionist statement. When you look at the Agbar Tower at night, the visual impact of its extraordinary skin is so striking that you almost forget its shape. (It's a reminder also that at night, lighting can turn any three-dimensional building shape into a very different kind of two-dimensional sign—something you can see in Texas skyscrapers outlined in neon or in Asian towers whose facades contain millions of tiny light-emitting diodes and act as gigantic television screens, perhaps the ultimate way of making a building's real shape seem, at least for a moment, irrelevant.)

Both the Foster tower in London and the Nouvel tower in Barcelona contain office space, so in neither building does the striking shape determine the nature of the interior, the way it does, say, at the Pantheon, or in I. M. Pei's pyramid at the Louvre, where the interior is mainly a hollowed-out version of the exterior shape. Instead, the insides of these towers consist of relatively conventional offices, many of which have curved or slanted walls—a case of complex functions fitted into a larger package. That's what architects do all the time, of course. Almost every building is to some extent a Rubik's Cube of structure and different kinds of interior spaces, all fitted into some kind of larger shape. Then again, the structure that has the most striking and compelling shape of any tall building in the twenty-first century, the CCTV tower in Beijing—less a tower than a square version of a donut, upended, with its top pulled out into a startling cantilevered corner—is, if you listen to its architects, Rem Koolhaas and Ole Scheeren of the Office for Metropolitan Architecture, just the natural result of the logical organization of its functions. The architects put the large, horizontal production studios on the ground, other shared facilities in the horizontal sections that bridge across the top, and various administrative offices that support production into the vertical sections where they can connect to both the top and the bottom. The building is vast—though it rises to only fifty-one stories, it has more floor space than any other office building in Asia—and while its shape may indeed allow the functional connections the architects claim, this startlingly complex, structurally daring, Escher-like form is obviously not the only way to fulfill this end, and it is certainly not the easiest one. There is something a bit disingenuous about staking a claim to function in a building as determinedly bizarre as this one. You know that it came to be in part because engineers could get it built, something that could not have happened a decade earlier.

But function is an elastic concept, and it is clear that the creation of a memorable building that would make CCTV known throughout the world was as much a part of this building's program as anything about its offices and production facilities. There is nothing wrong with this; architecture has been serving as an identifying logo for large and powerful institutions forever. The Parthenon, the Pantheon, Chartres, the Forbidden City, St. Peter's, the Kremlin, Versailles, the U.S. Capitol—the list is endless, and CCTV is hardly the first corporation to join it. The Woolworth Building, the RCA Building at Rockefeller Center, Johnson Wax, Lever House, and the Sears Tower are just some of the many that came before. The question this building raises is not whether it is appropriate for a corporation to want to be

Rem Koolhaas and Ole Scheeren, Office for Metropolitan Architecture,
CCTV headquarters, Beijing

known for a striking and unusual building but whether that building makes sense as a public presence in the city. Does it seem only strange and willfully arbitrary, the way the shape of the Hirshhorn Museum does? Or does the unusual shape of CCTV play a valid role in the cityscape?

In Beijing, it makes sense. The Beijing skyline is largely a confused jumble of mediocre buildings, not only undistinguished but largely indistinguishable. CCTV is the first truly memorable tall building in the city, and it has already begun to function like the Empire State Building in New York or the Sears Tower in Chicago or even, in some ways, like the Eiffel Tower in Paris, as the tall element that is visible from many parts of the city and can serve both as a symbol of the city and as an orienting device. The CCTV building has the added advantage of looking different from different directions, which makes it even more visually compelling. When you pass by the building on Beijing's elevated expressway or catch a glimpse of it down the street, you cannot take your eyes off of it, and there are not many buildings you can say that about.

A CCTV tower, where an enormously complicated set of functions is fit into an entirely new kind of architectural shape, is not the kind of thing that happens often. It's much easier to fit all the different functional demands of a building, just by the simple laws of geometry, into a building whose overall shape isn't something unusual like CCTV or a sphere or a pyramid or an obelisk but is more along the lines of a rectangle, with straight sides and a simple, slanted roof or a flat top. It's easier to build those shapes, too. And it is easier to fit them together into the combination of buildings that makes up a street or a town square. It is no surprise that most buildings end up as some form of rectangle.

How, then, does an architect assure that you and I will notice and remember them? Sometimes, of course, being noticed isn't what matters, but I will say more about that in chapter 7. For now, let me say only that often the aesthetics of a building come not from a single overall shape but from a combination of shapes—a vertical slab set atop a horizontal slab, say, as Gordon Bunshaft did in his pathbreaking Lever House in New York, where the vertical slab appeared to float slightly over the horizontal slab, which itself was set on columns so that it would appear to be floating above the ground. Or the composition of shapes Oscar Niemeyer made iconic in Brasilia, where he set a pair of identical slabs close together, making a conventional form seem unusual by doubling it and then had the combination play off against a horizontal section with a low dome and a reverse dome, sort of like a dish. Niemeyer's buildings loosely recall the combination of forms an international consortium of architects created for the United Nations in New York, where the swooping form of the General Assembly Building serves as a counterpoint to the large, flat slab of the Secretariat Building and the horizontal mass of the Conference Building. Or, to move away from large office buildings and to a set of smaller residential buildings, there is the combination of rectangles and squares that Charles Moore used in Sea Ranch, his condominium complex on the Pacific coast north of San Francisco, designed in the early 1960s with Donlyn Lyndon, William Turnbull, and Richard Whitaker. This cluster of buildings is at once a set of strong, sculptural masses set against the sea and a group of modest cottages alluding to the simple, natural architecture of the farm shed. At Sea Ranch, Moore managed to pull together what would later be thought of as opposing strands of American architecture—the desire to create abstract, sculpted mass and the desire to connect to history—into a strikingly beautiful composition. Sheds were not reproduced literally here, of course: roofs were pitched in just one direction to give the mass of each section a crisper, more modern feel; there are skylights and projecting bays, and the structures are sheathed in vertical redwood siding. Sea Ranch is a masterwork of graceful restraint, standing front and center on the cliffs overlooking the Pacific. No part of it would work without the whole—that, more than anything, is the lesson of this composition of boxy masses. Here, the language of everyday architecture makes a statement about the power of abstraction and, beyond that, about the capability of a single work of architecture to suggest both intimacy and monumentality.

When a building consists mainly of a single box, as so many do, and neither is there an unusual shape nor are there multiple shapes to play off against one another, how then to give it identity? In other words, how do you make a box distinctive? The answer lies in the fact that the sides of a box do not have to be blank. In fact, they rarely are. Exterior walls have windows and doors, and moldings and cornices, and every other possible kind of ornament. How these elements are arranged is often a more important act of composition than the creation of the building's shape or mass. The facade of a building can be dominated by windows, which we usually read as voids, or by walls, which we

Moore, Lyndon, Turnbull and Whitaker, Sea Ranch, California

read as solids. The solids can be plain and flat, or they can be richly decorated. A building's facade can seem like a thin membrane stretched tight across the structure, hiding the structure as a curtain might cover a wall with an even, decorative pattern, as Pei and Cobb did in the Hancock Tower in Boston. Or a facade can have depth and texture of its own, as in the reinforced concrete apartment towers that I. M. Pei built in the early 1960s, like Kips Bay Plaza and Silver Towers in New York and Society Hill Towers in Philadelphia. Or it can make the building's structure an aesthetic statement on its own, as Bruce Graham and Fazlur

Khan of Skidmore, Owings and Merrill did in the John Hancock Center in Chicago, where enormous X-braces across the facade provide variety for the eye, a reminder of the building's huge scale, and a sense of how the building is held up. In some ways the Hancock Center was following a long tradition in Chicago of using the facade of a tall building to reveal something about its underlying structure. Many early Chicago skyscrapers contained a three-part window—one wide section flanked by two narrow ones—in between structural columns, a pleasing rhythm in which the varying thicknesses of vertical lines made clear what was merely a division between windows and what was part of the structure of the building. The "Chicago window" was more than didactic, however; it was a compositional tool that different architects were able to use in dozens of ways.

Most Chicago skyscrapers were designed to emphasize the vertical—Louis Sullivan in particular created buildings that, though small by today's standards, appeared to soar, in large part because the vertical lines of their facades were stronger than any other element, even Sullivan's intricate and elegant ornamentation. Sullivan's facades were almost always three-part compositions, consisting of a relatively solid base of one or two stories, a main section containing eight or ten or more stories and strong vertical lines, and then an elaborate top with a rich cornice. In the early days of skyscraper design, the notion that the facade of a tower could be treated like a classical column with a base, shaft, and capital was something of an aesthetic breakthrough, since it represented a recognition that the design of a tall building

J. P. Gaynor, Haughwout Building, New York

required not only a new kind of engineering but a new sense of architectural aesthetics as well.

If architecture is composition, then composition can sometimes be pattern. Repetition does not always guarantee refinement—indeed, it often produces boredom. But in the Haughwout Building, one of the greatest of New York's remarkable inventory of nineteenth-century cast-iron industrial buildings, a single pattern of classical elements, repeated over five floors, yields a facade of extraordinary richness and harmony. It is worth looking hard at this building to figure out why it all works so well. No element here is new; J. P. Gaynor, the architect, invented nothing. It is all in how he put the pieces together: five stories of windows, each within an arch set on miniature Corinthian columns, or colonettes, and flanked by large Corinthian columns set on paneled bases. An entablature and balustrade sit atop each story, with a rich cornice atop the entire building.

What makes this one magic and so many other such facades that combine classical elements pedestrian? Here, the detailing is crisp and precise, and the depth exactly right to create a sense of texture and shadow, but never so much as to make the building look as if it is made of something other than metal and glass. (No one, in other words, could easily mistake the Haughwout Building for a structure carved of stone.) More notable still is the remarkable balance between the facade as a horizontal element and as a vertical one—this pattern, like a good plaid, reads now as horizontal, now as vertical. And the building itself feels like both a deep mass—a big block—and a skin stretched taught over interior volume. You can stare at this facade for hours and continue to see only richness in the classical dance its elements perform, over and over again.

Rudolf Arnheim has best analyzed our shared perceptions of buildings in his attempt to specify what shapes, proportions, and relations among parts give pleasure. In *The Dynamics of Architectural Form* he observes that "the dynamics of shape, color and movement is the decisive, although the least explored, factor of sensory perception," which is to say that the relation of forms and masses to each other is key to how we relate to them. To Arnheim, why some forms and masses relate well and others awkwardly is common sense. We are most comfortable where there is a clear but not simplistic order; where there is a balance between horizontal and vertical forces; where the interior of a building bears some clear relation to the exterior; where space is neither so undefined as to make our presence in it seem inconsequential and thus confusing or irrelevant nor so rigidly and tightly defined as to make us feel squeezed and oppressed by it.

Arnheim, who speaks of the horizontal as the "plane of action" and the vertical as the "plane of vision," brilliantly ties his observations about architecture to what might be called intuitive perception in general: "The ratio between rising and reposing, lightness and weight, independence and dependence, is at the very core of the human sense of what life is and ought to be, and as such it is a principle variable of style." It is all a matter, he concludes, of balance. Balance between light and heavy, close and near, tall and short, bright and dim, active and calm, not unlike Rasmussen's conclusion. Elements must be in scale with each other and with us. This could almost be a prescription for classical architecture, though to his credit, Arnheim makes no attempt to limit his principles to classicism or any other style.

Although few metaphors are more tired than that of architecture as music, it is difficult not to think of harmonic proportion in music in connection with balance in architecture. Visual balance is not so definable and measurable as musical harmony, but the sense of discord in its absence is every bit as marked. Elements must relate comfortably; they must appear to be cooperating, to be part of a larger order, in the composing of a facade in architecture as much as in the making of a musical sequence. Look, for example, at the facade of Alberti's great fifteenth-century church of Santa Maria Novella in Florence, where columns, arches, pilasters, volutes, and niches—a whole range of classical elements—are arranged to culminate in a pediment; every aspect of this brightly colored facade seems organized to bring your eye up and to give it a sense of pleasure and wholeness, just as a musical composition carries your ear along. Every element is part of a larger whole, and its place in that larger whole is essential, unmistakable, and unchangeable. Take anything away, and the facade no longer works. Add anything, and it seems excessive. All the elements seem to connect, and your eye follows easily from one to the next, but what you sense is not the parts but the whole. Now, to work this way hardly means that every part in an architectural composition must be quite as similar as Alberti's classical elements—indeed, if they are too much the same they risk being dull, as in, say, the bombastic attempts at classical architecture produced by Albert Speer for the Nazis or the dreary, bureaucratic architecture produced by twentieth-century governments of almost every political stripe. But an architectural composition rarely succeeds if the elements that make it up are so different that they appear to be in competition with one another. Severe discord can sometimes work to make a point, but it should not be a steady visual diet.

And too much plainness and too much order can be dull. Robert Venturi's *Complexity and Contradiction in Architecture* contained his famous retort to Mies van der Rohe's mantra of "Less is more": "Less is a bore." Venturi wrote this in 1966, and his book is often taken as a polemic along the lines of Le Corbusier's *Towards a New Architecture,* with Venturi playing Le Corbusier's opposite number, telling people not to reject history

Leon Battista Alberti, facade, Santa Maria Novella, Florence

but to look at it again and understand that it was never so simple as it was made out to be. "Architecture is necessarily complex and contradictory in its very inclusion of the traditional Vitruvian elements of commodity, firmness and delight," Venturi wrote. Venturi was actually less interested in offering up a retort to Le Corbusier and other modernist zealots than he was in arguing the aesthetics of architectural form and issuing a call for architecture to reflect "the richness and ambiguity of modern experience," which he felt that orthodox modern architecture, with its focus on minimalist simplicity, ignored. But through most of architectural history buildings have not been pure and consistent,

Venturi argued, and why should our time be different? Venturi said he wanted architecture to be "hybrid rather than 'pure,' compromising rather than 'clean,' distorted rather than 'straightforward,' ambiguous rather than 'articulated,' perverse as well as impersonal, boring as well as 'interesting,' conventional rather than 'designed,' accommodating rather than excluding, redundant rather than simple, vestigial as well as innovating, inconsistent and equivocal rather than direct and clear. I am for messy vitality over obvious unity. . . . I am for richness of meaning rather than clarity of meaning."

If literature and film and poetry and painting could reflect the ambiguities of modern life, why couldn't architecture, Venturi asked. He was right, of course. Architecture has never been as simple as the modernist ideologues would have it, and the best buildings, including the modernist ones, have never fit any mold. Venturi's book contains page after page of examples of buildings by Borromini and Bramante and Michelangelo and Nicholas Hawksmoor and Frank Furness and William Butterfield and Louis Sullivan and even Le Corbusier himself, all to make the point that architectural composition is a matter of inventiveness more than formula and that the greatest buildings often do the least expected things.

Surprise is essential, and although the notion of ordered surprise may appear to be an oxymoron, some degree of surprise is always going to be present in any work of architecture that has the capability to move you. When every element is predictable, order becomes a source not of comfort or serenity but of banality.

The building that works best is one in which there is something that is different enough from what might normally be done as to awaken us, even if we have seen it a hundred times before. The opening chords of Beethoven's Fifth Symphony or the sensuous forms amid color in Matisse's *The Dance* have something in common with Alberti's Santa Maria Novella, but also with the swooping arch of Louis Sullivan's Owatonna Bank in Minnesota and the delicate classical variations of Jefferson's pavilions at the University of Virginia. None of these buildings does things in quite the expected way, but each one evokes a startling instant of pleasure no matter how many times we have experienced it. So, too, with the crown of the Chrysler Building and the split pediment of Blenheim Palace in Oxfordshire and the stacking of spire atop tower atop arched portico of Hawksmoor's Christ Church, Spitalfields, or the overpowering top floor of Robert Smithson's Wollaton Hall, near Nottingham, the great Elizabethan country house; or the combination of a lyrical, curving facade facing the river and a sharply angular facade facing the city at Alvar Aalto's Baker House dormitory at the Massachusetts Institute of Technology; or the way the sumptuous and witty country villas of the great early-twentieth-century English architect Sir Edwin Lutyens manage to distort the classical tradition and to pay homage to it at the same time.

In every one of these buildings, the order of convention is combined with the magic of invention. What they give us is not just unexpected but right; it manages to be startling and yet still harmonious. We might say that it expands our sense of what harmony can mean. And that may be as good a definition as I can come up with for the balance to which all architecture must aspire: to be both familiar and new, to provide both pleasure and serenity, order and novelty, intensity and repose, somehow managing to make you feel both equilibrium and a sense of revelation, all at once.

4
architecture
as space

Space is "nothing"—a mere negation of the solid. And thus we come to overlook it. But though we may overlook it, space affects us and can control our spirit. . . . The architect models in space as a sculptor in clay. He designs his space as a work of art; that is, he attempts through its means to excite a certain mood in those who enter it.

GEOFFREY SCOTT, *The Architecture of Humanism*

When you think of a building as an object, you think about its overall shape, about the quality of its facade, and of how its other sides, if they are visible, read as compositions. You think of it as mass and volume and bulk. You see it in terms of line and color and materials. And you consider it in relation to the buildings around it.

But of course there is another dimension entirely to buildings, and that is the way they feel when you go inside them. Buildings are created to enclose space. The reality of architecture consists as much of space as form, and the nature and the feel of the space within a building can mean as much as anything else about the building, and sometimes more. Space can feel large and open, or it can feel small and confining. It also can feel large and disorienting or small and protective. It can be exhilarating or oppressive. It can feel generous or mean. It can feel clear or mysterious. It can feel soft or hard; a space that is carpeted and paneled in wood will treat you more gently than a space of exactly the same dimensions that has a terrazzo floor and solid walls. And the same holds true for light. A space can be light or dim; two rooms of the same size will feel altogether different if one has natural light and the other is lit artificially, and in the room with artificial light, there are infinite possibilities for varying the light, and each will change how you perceive the space. Not for nothing did someone invent the phrase "mood lighting." In a similar vein, one space can be festooned with ornament and another of the same size can be starkly pure, and they, too, will feel entirely different. A space can be as confusing and difficult to navigate as the maze of passages you follow if you are transferring between lines on the London Underground or as matter-of-fact as the perfect cube of the main hall of the Queen's House by Inigo Jones in Greenwich, England, which is roughly forty-five feet, seven inches high, forty-five feet, seven inches wide, and forty-five feet, seven inches deep. A high space can be as neatly articulated as the atrium of the Brown Palace Hotel in Denver, where the corridors on every floor take the form of balconies overlooking the big space, at once providing texture and a sense of scale. Imagine the atrium in the Brown Palace or in its most influential modern progeny, John Portman's Hyatt Regency in Atlanta, with nothing but plain solid walls. It would feel not uplifting but oppressive. The nine-story-high central space in the Brown Palace always seems to come on you as a surprise, which is part of its allure; you are not attuned to expect a huge, spectacular room in the middle of a stolid nineteenth-century hotel, and it is hard to suppress a sense of glee when you walk into it.

Whatever form it takes, interior space will almost always provoke a greater emotional response than the outside of a building does. Space can be directed, and feel as if it were created to encourage you to move through it, or it can be focused, and make you feel as if you do not need to move through it to understand it. The Beijing International Airport by Norman

Foster, which is laid out in the shape of a huge funnel, is not only a spectacular space with its high, swooping ceiling and generous natural light, it is a directional space, since the shape quite literally funnels you from the large entrance toward the security area and the gates. The Pantheon in Rome, the great circular temple, does not make you want to move through it, and you feel as if you understand it better if you stay put, under the perfect half-sphere of the enveloping dome. When you are in the Pantheon, you feel as if the world revolves around you; even if you are not in the very center of the great circle (actually, the space is better experienced from off-center), you feel as if the force of the space is focused on you, like a laser. You don't want to move. To move is to break the spell. What is supposed to move, you realize, is the light, which comes into the space through the oculus, the round opening that is at the very top of the dome, and lands on the floor in the form of a round disc of sun.

We talk about facades in terms of how they look; we talk about spaces in terms of how they feel. Great space—like the Unity Temple by Frank Lloyd Wright or Sir John Soane's breakfast room (see chapter 1) or Mies van der Rohe's Farnsworth House or Borromini's Sant'Ivo church—makes you feel something in the pit of your stomach. I don't know any other way to describe it. It is a sense of awe and contentment, somehow joined, and you feel as if you have been jolted into a higher level of perception than you normally have. If architecture is ever able to bring you to a state you might describe as resembling nirvana, it will almost surely be because of a space you are in, not because of a facade

Interior view, Pantheon, Rome

you are looking at. If it is difficult to quantify aesthetics, it is utterly impossible to quantify the experience of being in great architectural space. You feel amazement and curiosity, since you want to take the pieces apart in your head and figure out how the architect did it. But you also feel a serene pleasure in it exactly as it is, and you can go back and forth between trying to understand how it was put together and simply absorbing its intensity and letting it wash over you.

Even more conventional spaces create distinct physical sensations. As I said, some spaces feel directed and encourage movement, and others feel focused and make us want to stay in one place, just as some places make us feel compression and tightness while others make us feel relaxation and openness. Some spaces seem to pull you toward the center; others push you to the edges. A space with a lot of windows will almost always pull you toward the view, and sometimes it can even feel more like an open balcony facing a vista than an enclosed architectural space. When there is only glass, as in Philip Johnson's Glass House or Mies van der Rohe's Farnsworth House, the dividing line between inside and outside is unclear, and thus the space itself becomes deliberately ambiguous. Curiously, the ambiguity is far greater in Johnson's house, which sits directly on the ground, with the grass and trees at almost the same level as the floor, and your eye just carries your gaze across the glass. The Farnsworth House is elevated several steps above the ground and sits on a flat platform that has been designed to look almost as if it is floating a few feet above the earth. Nature is framed by this space, and you

Philip Johnson, interior view, Glass House, New Canaan, Connecticut

feel a clear sense of separation from it, even though the walls of glass mean that you are looking at it all the time. You do not feel anything like a normal sense of enclosure in the Farnsworth House, but neither do you feel exposed. The best way to describe it is to say that you feel anchored by the power of the frame, even as you float just above the level of the ground.

No two people respond to any architectural space in exactly the same way. A large space that exhilarates some people may leave others feeling adrift in the architectural equivalent of an open sea. A small space that creates an exciting tension for some

Eero Saarinen, interior view, TWA Terminal,
John F. Kennedy Airport, New York

can induce claustrophobia in others. I may find the swooping curves of Eero Saarinen's TWA Terminal at Kennedy Airport to be sensual and comforting as they swirl around. This building gives me a sense of sweet, low-key jubilance. You may walk into this same building and feel that you have stepped into a cartoon, architecture made for the Jetsons, and see only an oddly shaped curve above you, not a space that seems almost to dance. I find that the curving concrete vaults in the ceiling make me feel as if I am in a wonderful modernist tent; you may feel it is harsh and, for all its fancy swoops, silly and therefore unwelcoming.

To me, the main concourse of Grand Central Terminal is a kind of public square for New York, a railroad's gift to the city that is nearly a century old and, if anything, more inviting than ever. Here, Beaux-Arts architecture did what it did best, which was to use the traditional elements of classical and Renaissance architecture to create beautiful and noble public places. Grand Central is a vestibule to the city; here great space is used both to allow vast numbers of people to move through easily and also to enhance the ritual of arriving and leaving the city by housing it with appropriate ceremony. Grand Central is the city's symbolic front door, and it feels very different from, say, the Port Authority Bus Terminal or the current version of Pennsylvania Station, which is little more than a glorified subway station. When you come into the city through Grand Central, you feel from the moment that you step off the train that you are in a place that is capable of stirring your soul. You have arrived, and it is this extraordinary space that tells you so. For all its glory, however, the architects, Warren and Wetmore along with Reed and Stem, knew how to organize things, and Grand Central is almost as remarkable for the efficiency of its layout as for the beauty of its architecture.

Sometimes space can be spectacular and still difficult. The National Building Museum, which is in the old Pension Building in Washington, has a central space that is 316 feet long, 116 feet wide, and 159 feet high. It is punctuated by two rows of massive Corinthian columns, among the largest interior columns

Warren and Wetmore, and Reed and Stem, main concourse,
Grand Central Terminal, New York

in the world, which divide it into thirds. The room, which is really a covered courtyard, is stunning to behold, and as a space for a large party it puts every Washington ballroom to shame. It has a kind of nineteenth-century bombastic grandeur, the architectural equivalent of General Ulysses S. Grant astride his horse, rough-hewn but with brass buttons gleaming. Most of the events the museum holds in the space aren't big enough to fill it, however, and they tend to look like lonely remnants of something

Montgomery Meigs, National Building Museum, Washington, D.C.

larger, small crowds gathered in a space far too big for them. The very size of the space seems to swallow up almost everything, and nobody looks anything but puny beside those columns.

Space, in one sense, is just what is left over when the architect finishes building the structure. (That was literally the case with the Pension Building—the architect, General Montgomery Meigs, constructed an office building like a rectangular donut and put a roof over the hole, and he had his grand space.) Until the nineteenth century, architects tended not even to talk about space. They built rooms and courtyards and corridors, and halls and salons and vestibules, and what they talked about wasn't space as a concept in itself but what form the walls and the windows and the moldings and the ceilings took, since that is how they achieved the effects they were looking for. But that hardly means that space was just what happened to fall in between the walls. Although not all architects "model in space," to use Geoffrey Scott's term, the creation of a particular kind of space is often the driving force in creating a work of architecture. The quality of architectural space is never an accident. Space is shaped. Many architects conceptualize a particular kind of space first, and then create a structure that will allow it to be realized. Saarinen's primary motivation in the design of the TWA Terminal was almost surely the creation of a soaring interior space, and the vaulted concrete shell structure was his means of enabling it. Even more space-driven was Saarinen's design for the Ingalls Rink at Yale, where the whole point was to give an ice rink a high, swooping roof, setting it within a space that would seem by its very nature to symbolize movement. Saarinen was fond of quoting a Yale hockey player who said that when he skated down the ice and looked up at the concrete arch, it made him feel "Go, go, go." As for the TWA Terminal, Saarinen shaped the columns and the vaults to emphasize uplift. This is not an earthbound building, it is a structure that feels about to take off.

Saarinen believed he was creating a modern equivalent of Baroque space, which (even though Baroque architects never used the word "space") is complex and full of intensity. "The

Eero Saarinen, Ingalls Rink, Yale University, New Haven

Baroque architects were wrestling with the same problem of creating dynamic space," he said about the TWA building. "Within the limits of the classical order and their technology, they were trying to see how far they could go into a non-static architecture. At TWA, we tried to take the discipline imposed by the concrete shell vault and give it this non-static quality. In a sense, we were doing the same thing, only using different play-blocks."

It is striking that Saarinen used the phrase "non-static" to speak of Baroque architecture. The greatest Baroque spaces do not so much encourage you to move within them as appear to be in movement themselves; they take conventional spatial experience and bring it to the tenth power. How else to explain

Borromini? There are few spatial experiences more powerful than being inside either of his two small churches in Rome, Sant'Ivo and San Carlo alle Quattro Fontane, known as San Carlino. Borromini's "play-blocks," to use Saarinen's term, were the familiar classical elements of architecture—columns, entablatures running across the top of the columns, domes, and so forth. But he was obsessed with geometry, and he had the ability to take common forms and shapes and combine them in such a way as to produce extraordinary drama and surprise. The nave of San Carlino is roughly elliptical in shape, but its walls undulate, and it is lined with sixteen huge columns, almost too big for the room, which accentuate the feeling that the entire space is a dynamic presence. The columns support an entablature that runs all the way around the nave, reinforcing the sense of curvature; above that are four coffered half-domes, and above that is an elliptical dome, which resolves all of the intense activity below into a serene and even shape at the top—as good a metaphor as you could imagine for the notion of earthly pressure giving way to tranquillity in the heavens. "Space now seems hollowed out by the hand of a sculptor, walls are molded as if made of wax or clay," Nikolaus Pevsner has written of this building, and that is the key thing. Borromini took classical elements, which in the Renaissance were put together to emphasize pure, rational order, and arranged them in such a way as to create intense, fluid space.

Borromini did even more with geometric form at Sant'Ivo, a round chapel of extraordinary intricacy and power. Its layout plan is itself an achievement in geometry: Borromini started with a pair of triangles, one superimposed upside down over the other

Francesco Borromini, San Carlo alle Quattro Fontane, Rome

to form a six-pointed star. Three points of the star become semi-circular recesses, and three are polygonal, with a slight concave. Corinthian pilasters and a continuous entablature surround the space, giving it an even rhythm and supporting a high, slender dome that is made up not of a round drum but of vaults that carry all of the concave and convex lines straight up to the top, culminating in a circle that supports a lantern. Everything seems designed to thrust your eye upward, and it does. The all-white space, highly unusual for a seventeenth-century Baroque church, makes it feel even more abstract and modern. This is half Baroque church, half rocket ship. You look up, to the light, and to the fullness of this tight, narrow space within the dome, and you feel, quite literally, as if you are about to rise upward. I do not know that I have ever seen a better metaphor for the notion of

Francesco Borromini, Sant'Ivo, Rome

architecture and religious redemption. As you move through
Sant'Ivo you feel compression, release, and transcendence. Here
is the faith, manifest—faith in humanity as well as God, since the
real lesson of Sant'Ivo is that transcendence can come through
the careful and creative application of earthly truths. Every ingre-
dient Borromoni uses is visible and available to anyone. It is what
he does with them that makes this church so utterly sublime. At
Sant'Ivo, simple geometries are somehow combined to create a

work of architecture that embraces the deepest complexities of human imagination, a space that has at once the clarity of the Renaissance and the mystery of the Gothic.

The spatial quality of architecture is something you often begin to feel before you pass through the door. In an essay called "Whence and Whither: The Processional Element in Architecture," Philip Johnson wrote that what he called procession, the experience of moving through a building, was actually the most important element of all in architecture: "Architecture is surely not the design of space, certainly not the massing or organizing of volumes. These are auxiliary to the main point, which is the organization of procession. Architecture exists only in time."

Johnson exaggerated for rhetorical effect, of course, since he hardly believed that shape and massing were not important. But he was not wrong. Architecture does exist in real time, and our experience of it is frequently a function of our movement toward it and through it. Is there anyone who has not found the approach to the Taj Mahal as moving and as powerful as the building itself, if not more so? Or felt the sense of mounting drama as you walk down the center aisle of a church? And, to turn to everyday experience, think of the pleasure of approaching an attractive suburban house by walking from the street to the front door, as the facade looms larger with each step, the Taj Mahal experience in miniature. Most of the time today, sad to say, this experience is lost when people arrive by car and drive to the side or the rear, and more often than not enter through a garage and a back door, missing everything. Rare are the houses, even new ones, that are designed to accept the reality of the automobile not by putting it in a back or side garage and forcing everyone to use a back door but by a design that somehow makes the fact of arrival by car as a central idea, organizing a whole facade around automobile arrival so as to use it as a way to heighten rather than obscure architectural experience.

Frank Lloyd Wright had the notion of movement through his architecture always in mind. His characteristic low entrances were intended to give us a sense of compression, to make the sensation as you move into a larger space beyond the entrance all the more dramatic. That is why you enter the Guggenheim Museum not directly into Wright's extraordinary, seven-story-high rotunda but into a low vestibule, and only after that does Wright's great space reveal itself. Wright was nothing if not cinematic, and he designed always with an awareness of how people would move through his buildings and a desire to control that movement as best he could, like a director pacing the story as it unfolds. It is a lesson that General Meigs, architect of the Pension Building in Washington, never understood. The real problem with that space is that you pop right into it. There is no surprise, and nothing unfolds in stages. You go through the door, and then, boom—there you are, right under the 159-foot ceiling, with all that space sprawling out before you.

"The beauty consists in how you move into the space," Philip Johnson wrote, knowing more than Meigs. Johnson understood that we first experience architecture from afar, watch it change as we move closer, and have (if we are lucky) an experience of great drama as we move, step by step, into it. And then we see it in different ways again when we stand inside and move around within its spaces. Architecture reveals itself in stages as we move toward it, and then space unfolds in stages as we move within it.

We may talk about proportion and materials and scale and composition when we stand still and look at a building, but that is still fundamentally a two-dimensional experience. Space adds a third dimension, and movement through space brings yet another dimension to the experience, the fourth dimension of time. So does movement toward a building. The impact of some buildings is greatest at considerable distance—the Empire State Building is a more fully realized, beautiful form from several blocks away (or even from across the Hudson River) than it is when you stand at its own front door. I would rather see if from afar than from close by, and its interior is its least compelling aspect by far. (The most meaningful thing to do inside the Empire State Building is to look out from it: the building provides not so much any spatial experience in itself as a vantage point from which to view the entire city as if it were a single, vast work of architectural space.)

Chartres Cathedral exists in one form rising above the wheat fields of Beauce, in another as it commands the main square of the village of Chartres, and in still another when we enter its nave. First we see it as mass from afar, in the context of a regional landscape, with no sense of its texture or materials and only the most abstract impression of its shape; then, as part of a village, dominated by the form and feeling of its stone and its details now crisply and powerfully visible, and finally from within, as the light and color of the stained glass join with the stone vaults to define the nature of the space. Seeing Chartres in each of these ways is part of the experience of the building. All are necessary to understand it, and they need to be seen one after the other, as you move through space toward the cathedral.

It is hard to underestimate the importance of the connection between movement and architecture, even when you are not inside a building. A Baroque facade in Rome symbolizes movement even if you are standing still. Of course the point is not to stand still but to experience it as you move toward it. Indeed, you miss one of the best things about it if you are not conscious of how you approach it, which is almost always not on a grand, formal axis but quite suddenly, as a surprise: many of the greatest churches look as if they had been shoved into tiny piazzas, like enormous pieces of furniture, and you come upon them in an instant as you turn a corner. It is not just the beauty of the facade that strikes you but the way in which it springs upon you. One moment you are walking down a narrow, twisting street, and the next moment you are confronting overflowing architectural glory. A Baroque facade speaks of texture most of all—of curves, of depths and shadows, of decoration that is assertively three-dimensional. It is architecture of the highest order of sensuality. You may find that it wreaks of excess, or you may feel that it represents the closest that built form has come to representing ecstasy, but you are not likely to ignore it.

If architectural space connects inevitably to movement, a building's plan, its interior layout, is the guide to that movement. The floor plan is the building's map. It does not literally represent space, but it implies space. A plan, you might say, is a two-dimensional diagram of a building's three-dimensional reality. The plan of Sant'Ivo does not show you the extraordinary nature of Borromini's space, but it shows you the basis for his thinking, the beginning of his process of design, and you cannot begin to understand this complex and magnificent space without first understanding the plan. In a building of many rooms, the plan shows us the architect's ideas for how spaces are arranged and for what your experience will be as you move from one to the next. You can see from a plan how you enter and where you go from there: what choices you have when you move beyond the entrance, which spaces are major and which ones are minor, and how they all relate to one another. It shows that spaces have a hierarchy as well as a sequence. Some spaces are grand and public and ceremonial, others more intimate and social, and others purely utilitarian, and this is true whether you are talking about a split-level suburban house or the Vatican.

Floor plans are often the best way in which to trace the evolution of some types of architecture, such as apartment houses and office buildings. In the late nineteenth century, when the first large apartment houses were being built in the United States, they tended to have rooms strung out in rows or set along extended, narrow corridors, a fairly primitive arrangement that prevailed even in such grand buildings as the Dakota, Henry Hardenbergh's magnificent Manhattan structure of 1884. It wasn't until around World War I that architects figured out that it was much more graceful, not to mention efficient, to lay out apartment suites around a large foyer. The floor plans tell the story. Similarly, in the days before air conditioning, office buildings and hotels were laid out around courtyards and air shafts to assure that every occupant was close to a window; they had numerous small rooms and often long corridors that made complex turns. Many buildings had floor plans that looked like the letter "E." Today's office buildings have large, open floors, and hotels tend to be narrow, even slabs. The floor plans show it all.

At the École des Beaux-Arts in Paris, the great French academy that was, for all intents and purposes, the first true architectural school, the ability to create a clear, logical, and elegant plan was considered as important as any aspect of designing a building. The Beaux-Arts architects believed that from a good plan, other good elements logically flowed, and without a good plan, a building could not fully succeed, no matter how elegant its facade or extravagant its interior spaces. The plan was the basis of everything. It was the document that ordered the spaces in the architect's mind and translated that order and logic into the actual experience of being in a building. You can sometimes understand more about a building by looking at its plan than about anything else. A photograph of the facade or of the central rotunda of the National Gallery of Art in Washington by John Russell Pope (which is discussed further in chapter 6) will show you the austere classical grandeur of Pope's architecture, but a look at the floor plan will tell you something that goes even more to the essence of the building, which is how Pope organized it symmetrically around the rotunda as a series of galleries, set in sequence around wide corridors, with breaks for sunlit garden courts. It is serene and ordered yet full of variation, always clear and logical yet never boring. You cannot get lost here, as you can

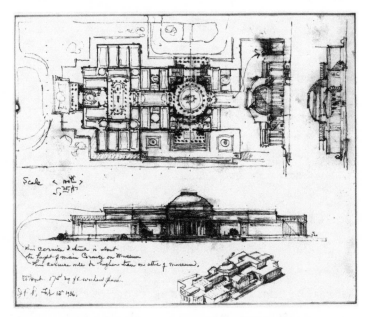

John Russell Pope, floor plan, National Gallery of Art, Washington, D.C.

at so many traditional museums, but neither are you likely to feel as if you are traipsing through room after identical room, with no relief. The floor plan explains it all, and when you look at it, you can see how Pope designed the building to encourage a sense of promenading through a sequence of galleries and to assure that visitors have the chance to vary their routes and yet never lose a sense of where they are.

Mies van der Rohe's floor plans, as in the Barcelona Pavilion, designed for the 1929 International Exhibition, show a sense of continuous space, punctuated by the brief lines of short walls; it is almost like an abstract composition. The plan of Le Corbusier's

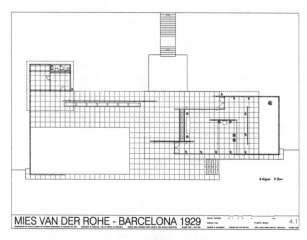

Mies van der Rohe, floor plan, Barcelona Pavilion

Villa Savoye helps you understand one of the critical elements of that great modernist house, the way in which curving walls play off against a rectangular frame. If you look at a floor plan for one of Frank Lloyd Wright's great early houses, such as the Ward Willets House in Highland Park, Illinois, of 1902, or the Robie House in Chicago, of 1909, you can see exactly what Wright was doing: opening up space, breaking apart the traditional rooms to make space seem to flow horizontally outward rather than to be focused inward. Yes, you can learn that from a photograph, too, but a photograph will not show you how Wright envisioned movement through the house. The plan will.

A plan is of little help, however, in understanding a building like Paul Rudolph's Art and Architecture Building (now Paul Rudolph Hall) at Yale, which I discuss in more detail in chapter 6. The building ostensibly has seven floors, but it really

Paul Rudolph, cutaway view, Art and Architecture Building
(now Paul Rudolph Hall), Yale University, New Haven

has roughly thirty-five levels, most of them small areas that are slightly up or down from one of the main floors. A section, which is a drawing of the building in a cutaway view, as if a knife had sliced through its middle, is the only diagram that makes much sense in this case. Rudolph was an architect who thought in three dimensions; like Sir John Soane, his spaces penetrated from one to the other, interconnecting vertically and horizontally in so many ways as to make the traditional idea of a room enclosed by four walls all but irrelevant. "The best architect is the one who knows how to waste space best," Rudolph said. His use of the word "waste" was slightly disingenuous, since he hardly thought he was tossing away space as useless. What he meant was that architecture should be measured not just in efficiency but in how creatively an architect could use space for aesthetic effect. Rudolph delighted in creating space that had a powerful emotional impact, and he almost always did it through compositions of straight lines, not through the fluid, voluptuous curves of his contemporary Eero Saarinen or of Frank Gehry a generation later. Louis Kahn similarly created great drama by brilliant arrangement of seemingly straightforward elements at the First Unitarian Church in Rochester, a building that seems rough, even cold, at first but that turns out to be profoundly spiritual, a magnificent joining of the softness of light to the hardness of concrete—or is it the hardness of light and the softness of concrete? It is Kahn's genius that allows us to experience it both ways.

Long before Kahn, in 1909 Frank Lloyd Wright made a composition of straight lines into an architectural drama of the highest order at Unity Temple, his Unitarian church in Oak Park, Illinois, its sanctuary a room that seems at once as protected as a cave and as open to nature as a tent. Unity Temple was helped, as was almost always the case in Wright's work, by a brilliantly controlled sequence of spatial experiences that take you across the building, down through a lower level, and then up into the glorious interior space. It is a movement toward openness and light, an ascension in every sense of the word.

It shouldn't be all that surprising that so many great architectural spaces have been created for religious purposes. Not only is a religious building a circumstance in which it seems justified to use space extravagantly, but the very nature of a spiritual quest would seem to transcend the usual limits on architectural creativity. Le Corbusier, in designing his chapel at Ronchamp, in eastern France—the building, completed in 1955, shocked many modernists with its use of curving, almost free-form shapes—spoke of "ineffable space" as being central to the mission of designing a place of worship. The building was criticized as "irrational" by Nikolaus Pevsner, who grudgingly noted, "Some visitors say that the effect is movingly mysterious."

Not only curving walls can yield "ineffable space." Tadao Ando's Church of the Light outside Osaka, Japan, of 1989, is a simple rectangle of smooth concrete, sliced through by a free-standing wall set at a fifteen-degree angle to the rectangle, as if it were a huge panel that had been swung on a hinge. The angled wall yields a small vestibule and an entrance to the chapel, which fills the rest of the rectangle. At the far end, facing the congregation, the wall is broken by an immense cross cut all the way through the concrete, so that light shines through. Light also enters from above the angled wall and through a large window positioned so that it looks into the angled wall, bringing reflected light onto the concrete. The room is crisp and clean, and the concrete has the beauty of fine plasterwork. But the room is not simple. The light and shadow join with the concrete to create something that feels at once rational and unexplainable— perhaps the most moving small chapel since Ronchamp.

In Gates of the Grove, a synagogue in East Hampton, New York, completed in 1989, Norman Jaffe created a sanctuary of wood, glass, and Jerusalem stone in which the whole idea of walls and ceilings is blurred. Jaffe designed walls in the form of great columns of wood that rise up, then slant backward forty-five degrees, then cross the room and descend on the other side, creating a series of great arcs. In between the arcs, but largely hidden, is glass, so that light enters the space from above, indirectly. It pays homage in a distant way to the old wooden synagogues of rural Poland, particularly on the outside. But it also has

Tadao Ando, Church of the Light, outside Osaka, Japan

a certain similarity to Wright's Unity Temple, not in appearance —the two buildings could not be more different—but in how in both buildings you feel a remarkable balance between openness and enclosure, between being free and exposed, and being nurtured and protected. The light enters from unusual places in both sanctuaries, and the indirect natural light helps to shape and mold the character of the space. Jaffe, like Wright, was able to make rectangular, orthogonal space have the intricacy and, even more important, the mystery of complex, organically shaped space. That is no small achievement—to take a rectangular or square room and give it the mysterious aura of something transcendent.

Norman Jaffe, Gates of the Grove (Jewish Center of the Hamptons),
East Hampton, New York

In the sanctuary of the synagogue, as in all great religious
buildings, something takes us a bit away from the secular life,
away from the rational. In this space Jaffe tried to create a physical echo of thought, of contemplation—a space in which light
tumbles in softly, from sources we cannot always see; space in
which physical support, too, is almost mysterious, with the odd
angles of the arcs over you, space in which color and texture seem
constantly to change in the light. The sanctuary is a room of
beautiful serenity, yet one of action and movement at the same
time. It pulls you forward; it holds you back. It seems to embrace
you as it leaves you to your privacy. It joins people together; it

encourages them to reflect in solitude. Like Sant'Ivo, Unity Temple, and Ronchamp, it is a product of rational thought, yet it seems somehow irrational, mysterious. Ultimately this is space that has been created to tell us that for all we know, there is something we do not know—something that we will never be able to understand.

5
architecture
and memory

The city, however, does not tell its
past, but contains it like the lines of
a hand, written in the corners of the
streets, the gratings of the windows,
the banisters of the steps, the
antennae of the lightning rods, the
poles of the flags, every segment
marked in turn with scratches,
indentations, scrolls.

ITALO CALVINO, *Invisible Cities*

This was the London of my
childhood, of my moods and my
awakenings: memories of Lambeth
in the spring; of trivial incidents
and things: of riding with mother
on top of a horse-bus trying to
touch lilac trees—of the many
coloured bus-tickets, orange, blue,

pink and green, that bestrewed the pavement where the trams and buses stopped . . . of melancholy Sundays and pale-faced parents and children escorting toy windmills and coloured balloons over Westminster Bridge.

From such trivia I believe my soul was born.

CHARLES CHAPLIN, *My Autobiography*

Visual perception plays an obvious role in how we respond to architecture—our inherent sense of such things as proportion and scale, and of the way some materials feel harsh and other materials feel soft, or how some shapes suggest openness and others enclosure. Most people experience these physical elements of a building in roughly similar ways—if a building feels big to me, it is not likely to feel cozy and intimate to you. I want to consider now, however, another aspect of architectural experience, one that is different for every one of us and much harder to quantify but that, in the end, is probably more important: the role of memory. We each have our memories of buildings and places, our experiences of architecture that we have lived in or worked in or traveled to see, our versions of Chaplin's trams and bus tickets and colored balloons over Westminster Bridge. These memories set a tone for the way we experience the new, since to a significant degree we perceive buildings that are new to us by how they fit into a worldview that is formed by the architecture we have seen before, even if we do not actively remember it.

It is natural to find comfort in the familiar. That doesn't mean that we necessarily want buildings to look like ones we have seen before—that's true for some people, of course, and it certainly helps to explain the fondness so many people have for new buildings that look like the architecture of the past. But memory doesn't have to demonstrate its power in such a literal fashion. Sometimes it is more a matter of what sort of general cultural upbringing you have had. A skyscraper means one thing to a person who grew up in the shadow of the Empire State Building and something altogether different to someone who grew up in Iceland—and one thing to a person who was taken to the top of the Empire State Building at age six, another to a person who never heard of it, and quite another to a person who yearned to visit it and never did. A person growing up in Japan may have a sense of private space as tiny, delicate, and very much to be cherished; someone who grew up in an Italian villa may perceive private space as a kind of boundless natural resource. The child who first experienced public space in the plaza of a Spanish town will have a sense of the public realm as a far more natural part of life than the child who grew up in Los Angeles, for whom public space was little more than a tiny playground, often reached by car rather than foot, and for whom the most significant experience of being in public consisted of riding in a closed car along the freeway.

We associate buildings with other buildings we remember or buildings we remember thinking about, which sometimes can loom larger in our minds than the ones we actually experienced. Sometimes the things we feel most attracted to are those we once aspired to and never had, architecture that exists, you might say, in the memory of dreams. On this notion Walt Disney invented Disneyland and built an empire. One of the most compelling images in the classic American film *Miracle on Thirty-fourth Street* is the magazine photograph of a house in the suburbs that a little girl who lives in a small city apartment keeps folded in her bedside drawer, her secret fantasy. (At the end of the film, of course, the girl moves into the house—not a house of the same general type but the very house in her picture, a twist of the plot that if nothing else sends the message that buildings are not, in fact, generic and interchangeable and that the ones that matter the most to us are real and very specific.)

Like the little girl, many of us react against our experience and feel attracted to buildings and places that are altogether different from ones we have known. The desire to seek what is counter to our memories exists not only in the case of people who grew up in cramped city apartments and crave suburban houses with huge expanses of lawn; there are also people who grew up in one culture who respond viscerally to the physical surroundings of another—Europeans who love Los Angeles, Americans who feel at home in Japan, and people from small towns anywhere who experience a quickening of the pulse whenever they approach a large city and who instinctively judge buildings at least as much by how close they are to a center of energy as by whether they provide light or quiet or a sense of serenity. To them, excitement *is* beauty, and if that idea seems to transcend the visual, think of Times Square, where to almost everyone visual excitement takes on a quality approaching beauty.

My own architectural memories are not unlike Chaplin's, a series of seemingly random, tiny images. I recall the buildings and the streets of my childhood intensely, but there was nothing terribly special about them. No architectural historian would give any of them a second glance. But that is, in part, the very reason they are worth recalling for a moment here, because of the way their ordinariness affected and shaped my architectural memory. The large public building I remember most clearly is my neighborhood elementary school, three elongated stories of orange brick, which in memory takes the form of a great Elizabethan manor house but which must surely have been much cruder. It had a modern addition, low and sleek in the manner of the early 1950s. I remember liking both the new and the old, and most of all the contrast between them. My eclectic sensibility must have been formed early. The new seemed so sleek and clean, the old so vast and shadowy; each was complete in itself, yet here they were literally jammed together. They both seemed altogether natural to me.

This little complex of school buildings marked one end of my immediate world; the other was a few blocks away, in the two-family house where my family lived on the first floor and my grandparents lived upstairs. The house had a tiny backyard and even less of a front yard, and it sat at the end of a long block of similar houses, houses that had a narrow side facing the street with a front door that nobody used except the mailman. Our house and every one of its neighbors was not very wide but quite deep, a kind of freestanding row house, not so different from the genre of houses in Queens that the world would later identify with Archie Bunker. The street was a place: I felt it then, even though I could hardly have articulated it. Each house was not so much a self-contained unit as a part of a larger whole, a box from which to view the opera of the street itself. We moved back and forth, up and down, house to house, yard to yard, playing sometimes in the street, more often on the sidewalk. The interiors belonged to us, to the private doings of our families; everything else was public, and it belonged to everyone.

I know that the sense of the street as a kind of public realm that I felt in the 1950s in a lower-middle-class neighborhood in Passaic, New Jersey, had something to do with the way I look at cities today. That part of Passaic was a rather miraculous kind of almost-suburb, balanced perfectly, if accidentally, between urban density and suburban sprawl. It had neither the roughness of the city nor the lushness of the country, but it was a perfect place for a child to see and feel for himself the qualities of a kind of urban village. I remember the street around the corner, lined with stores and a gas station (I did not know enough then to think of the gas station as a form of blight; I recall only the Esso "Happy Motoring" sign as being the first time I learned to read in script). The rounded corner entrance of Wilbern's Pharmacy, framed in black and chrome, and the classical dignity of the facade of the Bank of Passaic remain in my mind; so does the long soda fountain counter in Eleanor's candy store. And so does what must have been the most exciting local event in the years I lived in this neighborhood, a drama that also involved buildings: the dynamiting of a pair of two-family houses around the corner to make way for a new supermarket. The entire neighborhood gathered to watch the public spectacle, as striking a way of watching old architecture give way to new as any six-year-old would be likely to see a block away from his door.

If I was lucky to have spent my first years in a definable, measurable world, in scale with the feelings of a child, I was equally lucky in my house, a woefully ordinary piece of architecture, six rooms arranged more or less in a row, with no circulation space to speak of. For me it existed, in effect, in two versions: my family's flat downstairs and my grandparents' virtual duplicate above. But the two were the same in plan only, for our house bore the mark of my parents' early flirtation with modernism. They owned Knoll furniture, a platform couch and chairs of pale woods, whereas the flat above was rich and heavy, with deep upholstery, dark woods, and odd little things my grandmother called doilies all about. I could see that it was the same, and I could see that it was altogether different.

I could not have articulated this as a six-year-old, but it got through somehow, and my contention is that all of us see and feel and are shaped by the experience of early physical surroundings in a way that is not so different from what happened to me. We create from such specifics a kind of general sensibility. Can there by a better way to start thinking about architecture and cities than by growing up in a place that is as calm and ordinary as the one in which I began? It was a nurturing beginning, but not so comfortable as to have made me want to spend the rest of my life there (we moved away when I was eight, and I have never wanted to return), yet manageable and in scale with a child's reality. Would I have loved cities so much had I been raised in New

York? Would I have loved architecture so much had Chartres Cathedral been down the street? Would I have found majesty to be ordinary? Would my eye have been cursed as a result?

The familiar has a pernicious power; it can render glory banal. Familiarity does not really breed contempt, but it often breeds indifference, which is worse. Years after I had left Passaic I learned that something I had been seeing day after day, only a mile or so from our house, was one of the most remarkable, not to say bizarre, urban vistas in the world: a train track that ran down the middle of Main Avenue in downtown Passaic. It was a staggering sight—real trains, not trolleys, vast, noisy, magnificent objects rushing down tracks that ran right in front of the city's grandest stores, but to me it was routine, barely noticed, hardly remembered. It is startling only in memory.

So I was fortunate to have landed in this curious place between other places and thus to have learned, subliminally if not consciously, the virtues of ordinariness, the allure of urbanity, and the pleasures of small town and village life, simultaneously. There was enough urbanity to tempt, enough smallness to comfort and protect. And there were lessons, too, in the way that my grandparents' house upstairs was like ours downstairs yet not the same at all: even the least visual child could see how powerfully the different tastes of my parents and grandparents made the raw material of these outwardly identical rooms into separate and distinct worlds.

Before my age could be stated in double digits, we left Passaic and moved to a "real" suburb, Nutley, a nearby town where we lived in a medium-sized, shingled Queen Anne–style house with a splendid round porch of fieldstone; if this was not quite architecture with a capital A, it was a step up in the world from where we had been, and I could feel the difference in more than just bigger rooms and more space for running around. This house had a presence. It was complex, with attics and basements and funny little rooms and big triangular gables. My parents referred to it as "Victorian," and even though it was probably built just after the Victorian period, it definitely felt as if it had a history. I remember being told by my mother that the architect was William A. Lambert, which she believed gave the house a certain cachet; though Lambert was no Stanford White, he had built many of the best rambling, shingled houses in the area. I felt that the new house had the resonance of time, though I doubt that it was very much older than the house we had left.

Through our new house I began to sense the power of the individual building. I already felt the power of community, which gave me an advantage over many people with more purely suburban upbringings, who only later, if at all, grasp the importance of buildings coming together in groups to make a place. There was, of course, plenty of sense of place beyond my new house here, too, but I remember it all as disconnected, as things invariably are in towns where most movement takes place in automobiles. Franklin Avenue, the main street of town, a kind of stretched-out commercial strip out of *American Graffiti,* struggled to maintain some degree of urbanism against forces far greater than it, or the town, could cope with. It persisted, not quite a place for a promenade, but not entirely ruined by the malls outside of town either. The local supermarket survived by making itself more and more like a freestanding store, its owners tearing down everything on one side, and then on the other side, and finally across the street, to provide more parking. Eventually—I was long gone by then—it came to look like a cross between a warehouse and a mall, cut off entirely from the streets around it.

Yet this town taught me plenty beyond these negative examples. It had a glorious sense of village symbolism: a center with a town hall, firehouse, police headquarters, public library, and high school all clustered around the American community's true heart, a football field. I don't know a more perfect expression of the public realm this side of Philadelphia's City Hall, whose great tower anchors the center of the urban grid, a visible monument to civic order—unless it would be Siena, in Tuscany. I could not have known it at the time, but the way things were laid out in Nutley was rare for an American community, even for one whose history went back to before the automobile eviscerated the centers of most American towns and cities. In Nutley, the focal point of town wasn't a mall, and it wasn't a set of strip malls along a six-lane road. It was a street, and a square, and a football field. The architecture wasn't much, but the priorities were absolutely clear. No house, no business, no private institution took precedence over the needs of the people. The public realm possessed the heart of the town, unequivocally.

If Nutley was unusual in the way in which its layout made the quality of its town-ness so evident, it had another strange quality that served me well: it was balanced unintentionally, but perfectly, between isolation and connection to other places. Of the thirty thousand people who lived there, it seemed that half could have been in Nebraska, for all they felt connected to New York, a mere ten miles to the east. But there were also plenty of commuters, and their presence dusted the town with the sophistication of the urban region of which it was a part, even though it never fully took hold, and so the town was farther from New York in spirit than in fact. The consequence of this is that I grew up knowing something about a great city and something about life in a small town, never feeling fully a part of either, a mulatto of urban sensibility. The city had a tremendous allure for me, as it did for many suburban kids growing up in the 1960s, and part of the reason I found it appealing was no different from what every other suburban kid felt: it represented freedom, glamour, and escape from convention. But to me there was also a visceral excitement, a true physical thrill, in the buildings themselves, their size and shape and energy. This place was not only big and bad, it was also the Emerald City, aglow with beauty and bedazzlement. I obsessed over New York; it was where all things were possible, and architecture was the proof of its magical power.

The architecture I perceived as a kind of wholeness, an urban feeling, much more than a matter of specific buildings. I saw the city as one vast, complicated, enticing object, full of peaks and valleys and nooks and crannies, but one big, interlocking thing, a product of nature like Yellowstone or Yosemite as much as a serendipitous collection of man-made elements. Perhaps a better comparison would be to a huge interior, for it all felt set apart from nature: one enormous room that stretched on for miles in which one could escape from the smallness of the rest of the world. What I recall from long ago as the furnishings for this room are the hexagonal paving blocks around Central Park and the rock outcroppings within it, the walls of buildings defining the hard edges of the park, and the buildings tightly set along crowded streets, and the sense of monumentality in great museums and theaters and stores, and the subway, which played as big a role in defining my sense of what the city looked like as any piece of architecture. I have only the dimmest memories of the Empire State Building or Rockefeller Center, but I remember clearly walking past a hole and seeing a sign saying that this excavation was to become the Time-Life Building. Somehow I never managed to see Pennsylvania Station before it was destroyed in 1963, and since I entered the city through the grungy reaches around the Port Authority Bus Terminal and Times Square, I barely recall Grand Central at all. My introduction to New York was not a tour of its great architecture; it was the legacy of comfort provided by the idea of the street itself and by the notion that a city as a whole must be greater than the sum of its parts.

I had no idea that I was getting, more or less by osmosis, the ultimate urban lesson. All I knew was that the place felt right. I loved buildings and paid attention to them as I walked through the city, but I had no conscious sense that I was learning something essential about architecture when I sensed that New York's aura of wholeness, of coherence, was more powerful even than its great landmarks. There seemed to be nothing strange about coming to know and feel New York without as yet having seen the Brooklyn Bridge or Trinity Church or the New York Public Library. The essence of the city oozed from every street.

The Seagram Building and the Guggenheim Museum were only a few years old in those days, and the gargantuan transformation that postwar architecture would make to the fabric of the city was barely felt as the 1950s turned into the 1960s. Soon enough the glass boxes would come, and faster than anyone could have imagined, but at that point they were something of a novelty, and all the more pleasing for that. How wonderfully Mies van der Rohe's great Seagram Building played off against the masonry buildings that surrounded it and—as we learned only later, when they began to disappear—were its essential counterpoint. The city then was solid, literally solid in the sense of being made of masonry, and conceptually solid in the way it felt like an ordered ensemble of many buildings that still sang in more or less the same key. When I first began to know New York you never heard the expression "urban fabric," not because the idea did not exist but because it was taken so much for granted that no one had to say it. By the end of the 1960s things would be different, as glass boxes spread everywhere, not elegant ones like what Mies had created for Seagram, but cheap, tawdry imitations, and the tight physical form of the city fell into disarray. But that is a story for later. For now, New York served as a solid frame, a rock of Cartesian order, against which my sense of place could develop.

I don't want to suggest with all this talk of place and urban fabric that I had no interest in architecture itself. I was passionate about new buildings, so much so that I devoured any material I could find on architects and the structures of the early 1960s. Friends of my parents, perhaps perplexed by the extent of my obsession, decided not to fight it and in 1963 gave me a pair of gifts that would deepen my interest still further: a subscription to *Progressive Architecture* magazine and a monograph on the work of Eero Saarinen, who had died a year or so before. The first issue of the magazine that came had on its cover the Art and Architecture Building at Yale, by Paul Rudolph, which had just opened, the latest addition to the remarkable series of modern buildings Yale had commissioned over the past decade. The Saarinen book showed his designs for the Yale hockey rink and new dormitories. I decided pretty much then, at age thirteen, that I was going to Yale because I liked its buildings.

I eventually came up with some more reasonable, if less inventive, reasons for going to Yale, and I arrived in New Haven in the odd circumstance of having a lot of its famous new architecture firmly in my mind. I liked it just fine, but what really swept me away was not the new architecture I had seen in books but the part of the campus that modern architectural historians and critics had most disdained, the imitation Gothic and Georgian buildings of the first four decades of the century. Once again, the world was teaching lessons, but at Yale they reached me more directly than those I had learned in New York: I was entranced by the work of James Gamble Rogers, the architect who designed most of Yale's Gothic and Georgian architecture of the 1920s and 1930s. Rogers's determinedly nonideological stance, his avoidance of theory in favor of what can only be called intuitive design, was liberating. It was all right for architecture to be about feeling good, I suddenly realized; stage sets were not immoral. It was the perfect epiphany for a twenty-year-old who was just beginning to learn about empirical experience and only starting to trust his eye.

The architecture I came to admire at Yale arose from a strange combination of innocence and cynicism: a calculated, knowing, astonishingly skillful manipulation of historical elements for romantic effect. It was born of love for an institution and a belief that that love could best be expressed, and the institution's future best assured, by replicating the style of the architecture of great institutions and great places of the past, all the better to connect with what was so admired. Was this hopelessly naive or devilishly calculating? It seems, as I look back, to have been some of both. What confidence Yale had once had in architecture, to believe in its ability to connect to the past, even to inspire transcendence. What certainty that people would accept the idea of architecture as a kind of seance, as if it could lift them out of their current place and time and drop them into another one. And yet of course it was never so simple as that—the most striking thing of all about the Yale buildings is the extent to which they were intended not as an escape from the present but an enrichment of it. Rogers and Yale were not trying to deny the present; they were deeply proud of the modern technology they used to build these buildings and of the modernity of the university that these buildings served.

In the age of modernism's great ascendancy the Yale buildings had seemed merely simpleminded and pointless. To people who believed themselves to have serious architectural taste they were an embarrassment more than a source of pride. Yet they were clearly better than that, and I worked to learn why. They were remarkably well crafted and showed nearly flawless knowledge of proportion, scale, and texture. And they emerged from a certainty about what an institution wanted itself to be, all qualities that raised them considerably over most of the modernist buildings that followed them. A coherent idea, even a somewhat silly one, can lend tremendous power to the making of a place. And the reality of the Yale buildings, I discovered, was a great deal less silly than a lot of the thinking behind them. This is the truly important lesson I learned here: that form and scale and proportion and texture say far more about the success or failure of buildings than the stylistic associations we apply to them. Mass, scale, proportion, and texture, not to mention a building's relation to its surrounding context, the materials with which it is built, and the way it is used, all mean much more than style.

Vincent Scully has said that we perceive architecture in two ways—associatively and empathetically or, in other words, intellectually and emotionally. We make intellectual associations between buildings and other buildings, and we feel buildings as emotional presences. Most buildings affect us both ways, and certainly all great buildings must function in both of these categories, reminding us of other structures and their forms while also evoking certain deeper feelings. Superficially the makers of Yale's Gothic buildings—and of so many other historicist buildings elsewhere in America, classical, colonial, Tudor, Spanish, Mediterranean, and what-have-you—thought of their buildings associatively, for they were clearly reminiscent of other architecture. But for me the great discovery was that they really worked best empathetically, for their real ability is to make us feel pleasure and comfort in their presence.

Plenty of other buildings are important in my memory—Le Corbusier's chapel at Ronchamp, which I have visited only once, when I took an all-night journey to it as a student, looms largest, if only because getting to it was so much a pilgrimage—but ultimately it is the buildings we live with every day that do the most to shape our architectural memories. Their influence is not as dramatic as a visit to a cathedral, and only rarely do they give us the exhilarating glimpse of possibility that great works can offer. But if we are lucky, the buildings we live with surround us with a combination of stimulus and ease, of vibrancy and serenity, and their greatest gifts are conferred quietly, without our even knowing.

Architectural memory is not always personal, however, and it does not come only from the buildings we physically visit. Sometimes it is shared, and it can be shaped by the images of buildings we see in art, in photographs, on film, and on television. This shared architectural memory sometimes can be shaped not by an image at all but by words; much of our common cultural memory of architecture comes from the descriptive passages about buildings in novels. As for painters, Claude Monet has probably done more than any photographer, and perhaps more than any architectural historian, to create the image of Rouen Cathedral for many people; his extraordinary series of paintings is more powerful in memory than a visit to the cathedral itself. I am not sure that I would say the same for Canaletto's great paintings of Venice—epic though they are, they do not overshadow the reality of the city—but they surely play a role in establishing a kind of cultural memory, a shared architectural memory of Venice. Edward Hopper's paintings of American places, whether a city street or a storefront or a gas station on a country road, do much the same thing. For many people, the image of a lighthouse or a clapboard cottage that they carry in their minds is shaped by Hopper as much as by buildings they have seen—unless, that is, it is shaped by the dilapidated farmhouse in Andrew Wyeth's *Christina's World,* which may be the most replicated building ever painted. Charles Sheeler's paintings have had a less dramatic but more meaningful impact on our shared architectural memory of the American industrial landscape, rendering it powerful and giving it artistic coherence. The sense most of us have of the great factories of the Midwest is really Sheeler's, in the same way that the image most people have of Salisbury Cathedral is J. M. W. Turner's.

Photography does the same, only more so. Perhaps the most recognizable architectural image of the second half of the twentieth century is Julius Shulman's photograph of two women, elegantly dressed, sitting in the glass box of Pierre Koenig's Case Study House No. 22 cantilevered out over the Hollywood Hills. Here, modern architecture is sexy, it is dramatic, it is fresh, and it is elegant. It is an image that has come to convey the allure not only of Los Angeles but of modern architecture itself. But could we not say the same of Margaret Bourke-White's cele-

Edward Hopper, *Early Sunday Morning*

brated image of the gargoyles atop the Chrysler Building, in which she herself appears, perched on one of the gargoyles as she holds her camera? Or Paul Strand's great photograph of the side of the J. P. Morgan headquarters on Wall Street, a brilliant composition that seems to use architecture as a way of explaining all you need to know about the ice-cold power of capital. And almost every one of Berenice Abbott's great photographs of New York in the 1930s, or Atget's images of Paris, confers on us more shared architectural memory, this time not only one of single buildings but also of the way buildings come together to make a city.

Buildings enter our memories as characters in films; they are characters in novels, and they even play a role in cartoons. Would Charles Addams's characters have felt quite the same if they had lived in a Cape Cod cottage? Addams knew that an ornate,

Julius Shulman, *Case Study House #22*

Second Empire mansion, at once ramshackle and grandiose, could seem menacing, even terrifying. He took advantage of these associations and made them stronger still, so that now, we connect such houses in memory with his macabre characters. When you hear the phrase "haunted house," you picture a house like that, not a suburban split-level.

Alfred Hitchcock also exploited architectural style to enhance emotional impact in *North by Northwest,* but with a very different kind of architecture. The modern building in the penultimate scene of the movie, a spectacular house in the style of Frank Lloyd Wright, is dramatically cantilevered over a mountaintop; its very existence suggests tension and improbability. Its facades are largely of glass, and all that glass suggests transparency, but of course there is nothing but duplicity within—a lovely tweak at modernism's own duplicity, we might say—and the startling space becomes the setting for a showdown. The stark modernity of the structure, and indeed the fact that it is itself so visibly a work of structure, underscores a sense of modern architecture as thrilling, dangerous, and exotic. This scene would not have been the same had the mountaintop contained a rustic cabin instead of this modernist extravaganza.

In *The Fountainhead,* of course, the entire plot turns on architecture. Modern buildings—at least those of the hero, the vaguely Wrightian Howard Roark—are presented as noble, bold, and powerful statements of strength and integrity. Buildings in a more traditional style are weak, insipid copies, intended to represent nothing but cowardice. I am not sure, despite the determination of the set designers to make Roark's buildings seem

Still from Alfred Hitchcock's *North by Northwest*

glorious, that Ayn Rand's architectural values imprint themselves on the minds of most of the film's viewers—if they had, modern architecture would not still be a hard sell—but there is no question that this film has played a huge role in shaping what we might call our culture's collective architectural memory. So, too, with such classics as Fritz Lang's *Metropolis,* which more than any other film created the image of the high-rise city as a place of grim and terrifying power; *King Kong,* which confirmed the iconic role of the Empire State Building (which *An Affair to Remember* and *Sleepless in Seattle,* among other films, extended); Billy Wilder's *The Apartment,* which played on the contrast between the crisp, modernist world of postwar commercial New

Still from King Vidor's *The Fountainhead*

York and the intimate, almost cozy space of a private brownstone apartment; or *Ghostbusters,* in which the Art Moderne apartment building at 55 Central Park West becomes, every bit as much as the Addams Family house, a character in the story. And of course so many of Woody Allen's films, *Manhattan* most of all, make the city's architecture—or, more to the point, our romantic image of it—a vivid presence in the action. (In *Hannah and Her Sisters,* one of the characters even leads an architectural tour.)

The cinematic custom of the "establishing shot," an image of a physical setting shown at the beginning of a film or television show to establish its location, often acts simply by itself as a kind of imprint on architectural memory. The New York skyline is

surely as well known from this category of images as any other—
there are, after all, hundreds of New York establishing shots,
from all periods—but the same thing is true of all kinds of buildings and all kinds of places, whether it is the shots that show us
Minneapolis at the beginning of the old Mary Tyler Moore television show, or those of the *Cheers* bar in Boston, or the generi-
cally modern, sprawling suburban house of the Brady Bunch. In
each case, the nature of the architecture is no accident: there is
something particular about it that is necessary to allow the story
to move forward.

And this is every bit as true in literature. *Washington Square*
would have been different in more than title had Henry James
located it elsewhere. His description makes it clear that the house
as much as the people within it sets the tone for the novel:

> In Washington Square, where the Doctor built himself a hand-
> some, modern, wide-fronted house, with a big balcony before the
> drawing-room windows, and a flight of white marble steps ascending
> to a portal which was also faced with white marble. This structure,
> and many of its neighbors, which it exactly resembled, were sup-
> posed, forty years ago, to embody the last results of architectural sci-
> ence, and they remain to this day very solid and honorable dwellings.
> In front of them was the square, containing a considerable quantity
> of inexpensive vegetation, enclosed by a wooden paling, which in-
> creased its rural and accessible appearance; and round the corner was
> the more august precinct of the Fifth Avenue, taking its origin at this
> point with a spacious and confident air which already marked it for
> high destinies. I know not whether it is owing to the tenderness of
> early associations, but this portion of New York appears to many per-
> sons the most delectable. It has a kind of established repose which is
> not of frequent occurrence in other quarters of the long, shrill city.

In an age before film, passages like this were really the only way in which architecture could be presented in an extended manner that would go beyond the single, static image of a painting.

Architecture is vividly present in almost all of the writing of Edith Wharton, far beyond *The Decoration of Houses,* the nonfiction work that was her first full-length book. Wharton's architectural memories provide much of the context for many of her stories and novels and thus, in effect, become a part of our architectural memories, as her readers. Wharton's description of the upper Fifth Avenue mansion of Mrs. Manson Mingott in *The Age of Innocence* is one of the most memorable passages of architectural writing in fiction:

> [She] put the crowning touch to her audacities by building a large house of pale cream-coloured stone (when brown sandstone seemed as much the only wear as a frock-coat in the afternoon) in an inaccessible wilderness near the Central Park. . . . The cream-coloured house (supposed to be modelled on the private hotels of the Parisian aristocracy) was there as a visible proof of her moral courage; and she throned in it, among pre-Revolutionary furniture and souvenirs of the Tuileries of Louis Napoleon (where she had shone in her middle age), as placidly as if there were nothing peculiar in living above Thirty-fourth Street, or in having French windows that opened like doors instead of sashes that pulled up. . . .
>
> The burden of Mrs. Manson Mingott's flesh had long since made it impossible for her to go up and down stairs, and with characteristic independence she had made her reception rooms upstairs and established herself (in flagrant violation of all the New York proprieties) on the ground floor of her house; so that, as you sat in her sitting-room window with her, you caught (through a door that was always open, and a looped-back damask portière) the unexpected vista of a bedroom with a huge low bed upholstered like

a sofa, and a toilet-table with frivolous lace flounces and a gilt-framed mirror.

Her visitors were startled and fascinated by the foreignness of this arrangement, which recalled scenes in French fiction, and architectural incentives to immorality such as the simple American had never dreamed of. That was how women with lovers lived in the wicked old societies, in apartments with all the rooms on one floor, and all the indecent propinquities that their novels described.

Wharton describes another building that plays an important role in the story, an aloof country house on the Hudson River, this way:

People had always been told that the house at Skuytercliff was an Italian villa. Those who had never been to Italy believed it; so did some who had. . . . It was a large square wooden structure, with tongued and grooved walls painted pale green and white, a Corinthian portico, and fluted pilasters between the windows. From the high ground on which it stood a series of terraces bordered by balustrades and urns descended in the steel-engraving style to a small irregular lake with an asphalt edge overhung by rare weeping conifers. . . .

Against the uniform sheet of snow and the greyish winter sky the Italian villa loomed up rather grimly; even in summer it kept its distance, and the boldest coleus bed never ventured nearer than thirty feet from its awful front. Now, as Archer rang the bell, the long tinkle seemed to echo through a mausoleum; and the surprise of the butler who at length responded to the call was as great as though he had been summoned from his final sleep.

It is difficult not to think that for Wharton, architecture is destiny. She makes clear not only the connection between architectural form and social status but also the extent to which architecture can function, not merely as a static backdrop, but almost as an active force in the shaping, not to say the limiting, of a life:

> He knew that Mr. Welland . . . already had his eye on a newly built house in East Thirty-ninth Street. The neighborhood was thought remote, and the house was built in a ghastly greenish-yellow stone that the younger architects were beginning to employ as a protest against the brownstone of which the uniform hue coated New York like a cold chocolate sauce; but the plumbing was perfect. . . . The young man felt that his fate was sealed: for the rest of his life he would go up every evening between the cast-iron railings of that greenish-yellow doorstep, and pass through a Pompeian vestibule into a hall with a wainscoting of varnished yellow wood.

Perhaps the most telling, if oblique, architectural phrase of all in *The Age of Innocence,* however, is the brief line in which Newland Archer, the protagonist, speaks of how the character of people can often be hard to discern, but buildings tell you clearly what they are. "Everything must be labeled—but everybody is not," Archer says. Architecture reveals the intentions of its builders.

As with films, there is no end to the extent to which architecture plays an active role in literature and to the way in which writers' architectural memories begin to shape our own. "In 1902 Father built a house at the crest of the Broadview Avenue hill in New Rochelle, New York," is how E. L. Doctorow opens *Ragtime.* "It was a three-story brown shingle with dormers, bay windows and a screened porch. Striped awnings shaded the windows. The family took possession of this stout manse on a sunny day in June and it seemed for some years thereafter that all their days would be warm and fair"—architecture setting a tone altogether opposite, you might say, from that of Edith Wharton or, for that matter, Charles Addams.

John Knowles opened his staple of high school English reading lists, *A Separate Peace,* with a description of a New England prep school that was far more engaging and illuminating than the novel's plot:

> I went back to the Devon School not long ago, and found it looking oddly newer than when I was a student there fifteen years before. It seemed more sedate than I remembered it, more perpendicular and strait-laced, with narrower windows and shinier woodwork, as though a coat of varnish had been put over everything for better preservation. . . .
>
> I didn't entirely like this glossy new surface, because it made the school look like a museum, and that's exactly what it was to me, and what I did not want it to be. In the deep, tacit way in which feeling becomes stronger than thought, I had always felt that the Devon School came into existence the day I entered it, was vibrantly real while I was a student there, and then blinked out like a candle the day I left.
>
> Now here it was after all, preserved by some considerate hand with varnish and wax. . . .
>
> I walked along Gilman Street, the best street in town. The houses were as handsome and as unusual as I remembered. Clever modernizations of old Colonial manses, extensions in Victorian wood, capacious Greek Revival temples lined the street, as impressive and just as forbidding as ever. I had rarely seen anyone go into one of them, or anyone playing on a lawn, or even an open window. Today with their failing ivy and stripped, moaning trees, the houses looked both more elegant and more lifeless than ever.
>
> Like all old, good schools, Devon did not stand isolated behind walls and gates but emerged naturally from the town which had

produced it. So there was no sudden moment of encounter as I approached it; the houses along Gilman Street began to look more defensive, which meant that I was near the school, and then more exhausted, which meant that I was in it.

In W. G. Sebald's *Austerlitz,* architectural memory is, as much as anything, the novel's theme. The book is full of remarkable passages of description—it is almost a continuous flow of images of place, and it begins with a scene in which the narrator comes upon a backpacker named Austerlitz in the waiting room of the train station in Antwerp "making notes and sketches obviously relating to the room where we were both sitting—a magnificent hall more suitable, to my mind, for a state ceremony than as a place to wait for the next connection to Paris or Oostende—for when he was not actually writing something down his glance often dwelt on the row of windows, the fluted pilasters, and other structural details of the waiting room." Sebald goes on:

When I finally went over to Austerlitz with a question about his obvious interest in the waiting room, he was not at all surprised by my direct approach but answered me at once, without the slightest hesitation, as I have variously found since that solitary travelers, who so often pass days on end in uninterrupted silence, are glad to be spoken to. . . . Our Antwerp conversations, as he sometimes called them later, turned primarily on architectural history, in accordance with his own astonishing professional expertise, and it was the subject we discussed that evening as we sat together until nearly midnight in the restaurant facing the waiting room on the other side of the great domed hall. The few guests still lingering at that late hour one by one deserted the buffet, which was constructed like a mirror image of the waiting room, until we were left alone with a solitary man drinking Fernet and the barmaid, who sat enthroned on a stool behind the counter, legs crossed, filing her nails with complete devotion and concentration. Austerlitz commented in passing of this lady, whose peroxide-blond hair was piled up into a sort of bird's nest, that she was the goddess of time past. And on the wall behind her, under the lion crest of the kingdom of Belgium, there was indeed a mighty clock, the dominating feature of the buffet, with a hand some six feet long traveling round a dial which had once been gilded, but was now blackened by railway soot and tobacco smoke. . . . Towards the end of the nineteenth century, Austerlitz began, in reply to my question about the history of the building of the Antwerp station, when Belgium, a little patch of yellowish gray barely visible on the map of the world, spread its sphere of influence to the African continent with its colonial enterprises. . . . It was the personal wish of King Leopold, under whose auspices such apparently inexorable progress was being made, that the money suddenly and abundantly available should be used to erect public buildings which would bring international renown to his aspiring state. One of the projects thus initiated by the highest authority in the land was the central station of the Flemish metropolis, where we are sitting now, said Austerlitz; designed by Louis Delacenserie, it was inaugurated in the summer of 1905, after ten years of planning and building, in the presence of the King himself. The model Leopold had recommended to his architect was the new railway station of Lucerne, where he had been particularly struck by the concept of the dome, so dramatically exceeding the usual modest height of railway buildings, a concept realized by Delacenserie in his own design, which was inspired by the Pantheon in Rome, in such stupendous fashion that even today, said Austerlitz, exactly as the architect intended when we step into the entrance hall we are seized by a sense of being beyond the profane, in a cathedral consecrated to international traffic and trade. Delacenserie borrowed the main elements of his monumental structure from the palaces of the Italian Renaissance, but he also struck Byzantine and Moorish notes, and perhaps when I arrived, said Austerlitz, I myself had noticed the round gray and white granite turrets, the sole purpose of which was to arouse medieval associations in the minds of railway passengers.

And finally, another great observer of place, the novelist Alison Lurie, describes a young couple's arrival in Los Angeles in *The Nowhere City*:

All the houses on the street were made of stucco in ice-cream colours: vanilla, lemon, raspberry, and orange sherbet. Moulded in a variety of shapes and set down one next to the other along the block, behind plots of flowers much larger and brighter than life, they looked like the stage set for some lavish comic opera. . . .

But Katherine refused to be pleased. She wouldn't even open her eyes to see this warm, bright, extraordinary city. She behaved as if he had deliberately set out to make her unhappy by coming here— as if his professional career had nothing to do with it.

. . . A dozen architectural styles were represented in painted stucco: there were little Spanish haciendas with red tiled roofs; English country cottages, all beams and mullioned windows; a pink Swiss chalet; and even a tiny French chateau, the pointed towers of which seemed to be made of pistachio ice cream.

The energy of all this invention both amused and delighted Paul. Back East, only the very rich dared to build with such variety: castles on the Hudson, Greek temples in the south. Everyone else had to live on streets of nearly identical brick or wooden boxes, like so many boxes of soap and sardines. Why shouldn't people build their houses in the shape of pagodas, their grocery stores in the shape of Turkish baths, and their restaurants like boats and hats, if they wanted to? Let them build, and tear down and build again; let them experiment. Anyone who can only see that some of the experiments are "vulgar" should look into the derivation of that word. He liked to think of this city as the last American frontier.

In *The Nowhere City,* architecture again becomes vastly more than background, more even than background elegantly described. It defines sensibility and becomes a metaphor for issues in a marriage. We quickly see that Katherine has one set of architectural memories and Paul another; and while their architectural memories could seem compatible in the environment of the East Coast, their differences move into high relief against the backdrop of Los Angeles. Lurie's view of Los Angeles as a loose, vaguely funky environment of exuberant popular culture is, in its way, as outdated now as Edith Wharton's view of New York, but that in no way diminishes its literary strength. In Wharton and Lurie, as in James, Sebald, and so many other writers, painters, photographers, and filmmakers, architecture strikes a powerful emotional chord that plays a significant role in shaping a work of art—and that, in turn, creates an entirely new dimension of architectural memory for us all.

6
buildings

and time

I suppose that all architecture has to die before it can touch the historical imagination.

SIR JOHN SUMMERSON,
The Unromantic Castle

In a city, time becomes visible.

LEWIS MUMFORD

Because we live with buildings, and see them all the time, our relationship to them is at once more intimate and more distant than our relationship to music or painting or literature or film, things that we experience episodically but intensely. When you are watching a film, your world consists almost entirely of what you see on the screen; when you are in a building, only occasionally do other perceptions and other thoughts disappear from your mind. I spoke in chapter 2 about the extent to which architecture, even good architecture, can encourage complacency; because we see it every day, as a back-drop to our lives, it is easy to stop seeing it with fresh eyes, however closely we interact with it. The complacency that time induces has a purpose: it lets us tolerate things that would be intolerable if we continued to feel them intensely. Thus you numb yourself to that awful shopping mall on the way to work, or you no longer grit your teeth when you see the ugly new storefront that replaced the beloved old soda fountain on Main Street. But such tolerance comes at a price—there is a high tariff to the comfort of familiarity, for it encourages us to stop seeing.

Our relationship to almost every building changes over time, and for all kinds of reasons. A building that seemed large and imposing when you were a child—say, your elementary school—

can seem small and ordinary when you return to it later in life. A building that held no interest whatsoever—perhaps a church or a hospital or an office tower—can seem vastly more significant, and perhaps even more attractive, if your life begins to intersect with it in a new way. Buildings that seem striking, shocking, bizarre, or merely different when new become more and more familiar over time, and you can move in your view of them from surprised irritation to acceptance, and sometimes even beyond that to admiration or joy. Like many people I first thought the buildings of Morris Lapidus, the architect famous for his glitzy Miami Beach hotels like the Fontainebleau, the Eden Roc, and the Americana, to be silly, even vulgar. In time, I think I began to see architecture in a less puritanical way and came to find them entertaining, and perhaps even more than that. Lapidus was not a great architect, but he was a very good one, and behind his panache was serious architectural skill, set off by wit.

So the first reason that buildings change over time is that we change. None of us is constant; we see the world at least a little bit differently every day, and changes in your feelings about almost anything can play out in the attitudes you have toward the architecture you see. You can become more sophisticated, you can become more impatient; you can become more desirous of privacy and quiet; you can become more stimulated by excitement and grandeur. A single building—whether a cathedral or a house—can sometimes affect you so profoundly that it changes your attitude toward all the architecture you see.

Then, of course, buildings themselves change. They are altered or expanded or repainted or given cute red shutters or whole new facades of glass, or they get new next-door neighbors that clash with them or lose neighbors that don't. When a skyscraper goes up next to a brownstone row house, the row house no longer looks the same, even if not a stone in it has been touched. Our relationship to these buildings is no longer the same because in some meaningful way the buildings themselves are no longer the same.

More important than either one of these ways of changing how we see buildings is a third kind of change, which is when the culture changes, when we begin to see buildings in a different milieu—when times have changed, we might say. This is the hardest kind of change to understand, but it is in many ways the most consequential and surely the most complex. Every building exists within a social and cultural context, and receives much of its meaning from it, and that backdrop is not static, either. Indeed, the culture within which you see a building is likely to change more often, and more completely, than your own eye ever will.

My own experience with the towers of the World Trade Center in New York went through several clear and very distinct stages, though to be sure it never reached the stage of admiration. It began with a phase that would be much better characterized as Resentment: what, I wondered, was this thing, or this pair of things, doing in the middle of Manhattan, so big, so banal, so unthinkably intrusive, all the more insulting because it is taking away the title of tallest building that I, like so many New Yorkers, believed rightfully belonged to the Empire State Building. Over the years that evolved into a second phase, which I could call Acceptance, or perhaps Grudging Acceptance, coming from, first, a recognition that we do, after all, get used to anything and that in the case of architecture we had better get used to it, because unlike a work of art or literature or music that we don't like, we may well see a work of architecture every day. Some other factors heightened my acceptance of the twin towers and made it somewhat more than just a matter of getting used to them. First, I came to recognize that these buildings did have a certain value as minimalist sculpture. The boxy forms played off well against each other, since one of the few things the architect Minoru Yamasaki did was to place them correctly vis-à-vis one another, not side by side but with the corners almost but not exactly touching. And their facades were largely of metal, not glass, and that meant that they did wonderful things in the light; they reflected the warm sunlight of dawn and dusk especially well, but at all times they shimmered, and their texture gave them a richness that people did come to value.

The twin towers had a weird mix of delicacy and bombast, and they tended to appear fragile and overbearing at the same time, admittedly a strange combination of qualities in a single building. Since they were the tallest things around, they also functioned as a kind of campanile, an enormous bell tower, two bell towers actually, in Lower Manhattan, and I came to value them for this as well. The towers became a kind of orienting device, which integrated them into the daily life of the city and made them more benign.

But nothing in this Acceptance phase reached the level of Admiration, at least not for me: the architecture was still too big,

Minoru Yamasaki, World Trade Center towers, New York

too dumb, too indifferent to the needs of the urban context of Lower Manhattan. Of course all of these views became altogether irrelevant when the extraordinary and horrific events of September 11, 2001, occurred, and conventional issues of architectural criticism were rendered moot. My feelings about the World Trade Center and just about everyone else's all became the same: the buildings became our first skyscraper martyrs. That evolving feelings about a building could culminate in this—a final phase, of architectural martyrdom—could not ever, of course, have been imagined, and it is surely like no other course of feelings about any building. We are not accustomed to thinking of any buildings as martyrs, but the World Trade Center is now inexplicably bound up in a whole set of other values that martyrdom embraces—if you doubt it, think of how, as I said in chapter 2, sidewalk vendors all over New York were selling pictures of the twin towers for years after September 11, the way they used to sell pictures of Malcolm X or John F. Kennedy. (These tragic events put this building, so little respected by architectural historians and critics during its lifetime, essentially out of the range of normal architectural criticism. Martyrs, after all, are beyond criticism. Joan of Arc was not a very nice woman, but you will not hear anyone ever say that. And few people dare to say anymore that the World Trade Center was not a very nice building.)

The towers of the World Trade Center symbolized modernity, both to the tourists who flocked to them and to the terrorists who attacked them. The fact that their symbolic power came more from vast size than architectural quality is beside the point. Paradoxically, the towers represented an ideal of modernity that seemed to communicate most effectively to people who were not particularly interested in modernity, if not outright hostile to it. Their hugeness and simplicity made them almost a cartoon version of gargantuan modern architecture—and as such, all the more attractive to tourists, who took pleasure in riding to the top of the buildings, and all the more pernicious to those who saw in them all of the evils of modern culture.

This is not the place in which to talk at length about society's complex and often contradictory attitudes toward modernism, which could be a book in itself. But it would be useful to say a word here about another important modernist building, less well known than the World Trade Center but far superior as a work of architecture, that was hailed when it was completed, fell almost immediately into disfavor, and eventually was restored to its role as a major architectural monument. The building is the Art and Architecture Building at Yale University, designed by Paul Rudolph and completed in 1963. It is a heavy structure of rough concrete and glass, arranged into a strong composition almost perfectly balanced between vertical and horizontal and solid and void. Most of the building's solid walls are made of a rough concrete that has been set in alternately smooth and rough striations so that it looks almost like corduroy. It is a building that has strong echoes of Frank Lloyd Wright's Larkin Building of 1904, his monumental office building in Buffalo, quite heartlessly demolished more than half a century ago. But it also owes a debt to Le Corbusier's monastery at Latourette, France, of 1955, the building that is generally acknowledged to have been the first masterwork of the tough, raw style that became known as Brutalism. One writer referred to Rudolph's building as looking like a train crash between Wright and Le Corbusier, though it could more kindly be described as a remarkable synthesis of influences from two very different modernist predecessors. It is a difficult building, but an exceptionally powerful and beautifully composed one, and it is easy to see how in the early 1960s, as glass boxes were beginning to feel all too common, Rudolph seemed to be showing a way toward a new kind of modern architecture, one that absorbed influences from its modernist forebears and used them to push architecture forward.

What the Art and Architecture Building was not was what you would call user-friendly. The building's harshness, which

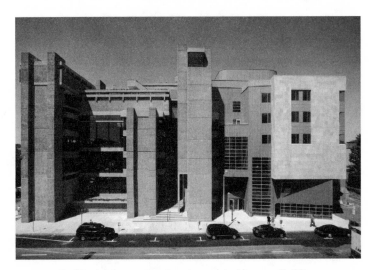

Paul Rudolph, exterior view, Art and Architecture Building
(now Paul Rudolph Hall), left; at right, addition by
Charles Gwathmey and Robert Siegel, Jeffrey Loria Hall,
Yale University, New Haven

extended to its multistoried open spaces, covered in bright orange carpeting and lit with bare bulbs, left many people uncom-
fortable. Sir Nikolaus Pevsner was invited to give the dedica-
tion speech, and he left no doubt that he did not approve of
the building he was dedicating: to him, it was an affectation, a
sculptural indulgence instead of the austere modernism Pevsner
favored. Taking note of the fact that Paul Rudolph was the chair-
man of the Yale architecture department, Pevsner told the au-
dience it was essential to remember that the client was the architect, and the architect was the client—in other words, if you don't
like it, there is only one person to blame. Less than two years

later Rudolph resigned and was replaced by Charles Moore, an architect whose work was lighthearted and playful, altogether different in tone. The first stirrings of postmodernism, an architectural style that sought to move beyond modernism by integrating elements from historical architectural styles, were in the air, and Moore was a major proponent of it. He made no secret of the fact that the building he had inherited was not his idea of what a school of architecture, or any other building for that matter, should look like, and he encouraged unsympathetic renovations. In 1969 the building was damaged by fire, and the repairs that followed changed it further. By the 1970s, Rudolph's design had been significantly altered, and not for the better.

By the 1980s, when the building entered its third decade, it was grudgingly tolerated as a battle-scared relic of an age of heroic modernism that was felt to be long gone. But the next twenty years would show at least as much of a swing of the pendulum as the previous twenty. Postmodernism sputtered, and the spate of historical revivals that emerged in its wake was beginning to seem less convincing, or at least boringly familiar. More architects, particularly younger ones, were coming to feel a renewed interest in modernist architecture, which, after all, was increasingly becoming a historical style itself. By the beginning of the twenty-first century, much of the most important architecture being designed was by architects who identified themselves as modernists. They wanted to invent new things in the modernist vocabulary, not to copy the work of a previous generation, and to them, the carefully composed abstractions of Rudolph's building looked not overbearing but appealing, even inspiring. In

2008 Yale restored the building to its original appearance, even down to reproducing the original orange carpeting, renamed it Paul Rudolph Hall, and added a new wing designed by one of Rudolph's best-known students, Charles Gwathmey.

What does it all prove? The saga of Paul Rudolph's building at Yale means more, I think, than the notion that everything that is old becomes new again. It tells us also, as the British architectural historian Sir John Summerson pointed out, that architecture almost always has to fall into disfavor before it can be appreciated on the scale of history. A building can attract all the attention in the world when it is new, as Rudolph's did—it was the equivalent in its day of Frank Gehry's Guggenheim Museum Bilbao in ours—but that proves only that it is capable of creating a certain level of excitement. It is new and different, visually compelling and full of ideas worth talking about. And talking about it becomes, in a sense, the latest fashion, which doesn't mean the building isn't capable of being more than this season's trendy event. It just means we can't know for a while. Fashion is what happens in the short run. Art is more of a proposition for the long run. Only after a building has emerged from the hoopla that surrounds its emergence as an object of fashion can we see if it has the qualities that will give it lasting importance. And almost inevitably what comes after a debut that defines a building as fashionable is for it to become unfashionable. There is almost always a reaction against adoration, even if only temporary.

This is true not only for buildings but for entire careers. The reputation of Frank Lloyd Wright, the most important architect the United States has ever produced, was at a low point for a generation after his death in 1959; it took at least twenty years for architects and historians to feel enough distance from Wright to look at him objectively. Today there is more Wright scholarship than ever, but there was relatively little attention paid to him in the years after his death. It took well into the twentieth century for Sir John Soane, who died in 1837, to be recognized as one of the greatest English architects of all time. (Soane, proud and cantankerous, did not leave behind a huge cadre of warm admirers, which surely didn't help.) And in our own time there was a significant reaction against Michael Graves, who in the early 1980s produced a series of buildings in a highly personal style that you might call a hybrid of classicism and Cubism. In the early years of postmodernism, Graves was all the rage—not only did his buildings get lots of attention, Graves himself became one of the first celebrity architects. Then fashion moved on, and Graves didn't. Graves, like Paul Rudolph a generation before him, has stuck to his guns, and continues to produce work in the style that made him famous, because, also like Rudolph, he believes in it. There may well be a Graves revival as there has been a Rudolph one.

To say that it takes time to determine the significance of a work of architecture—that time will tell, as it were—is not to say that great works do not bear the mark of their time, that they are "timeless." Nothing is timeless. Everything tells us something about the age in which it was made and in some way signals us as to what that age was. One of the things that characterizes great or even very good architecture is that it has meaning that lasts far beyond its time, but that is not the same as saying that it transcends its time. It may have qualities that transcend the immediacy of its moment, and it may communicate eloquently to people living in different times from the one in which it was created. Indeed, it has to do that if it is going to be more than fashion. But that hardly denies the fact that every work of architecture, from the most ordinary to the most transcendent, has roots in a particular time.

As the modern movement was developing in the late nineteenth and early twentieth centuries, its staunchest polemicists, such as Le Corbusier, made much of the idea that there was a "style for the time," as we saw in chapter 1. The argument was that you could make architecture either in the true way that was faithful to the concerns of the moment or in the false way that was not. To build in the wrong way was to do what the nineteenth century did, which was to make architecture that resembled some style of the past—Gothic, classical, Romanesque, Italian Renaissance, Georgian, and so forth. To build in the right way was to be inspired by the age of the machine and to turn away from the historical styles that to the modernists were just so much clutter. There was a lot of rhetoric about a new age needing a new architecture. (In Frank Lloyd Wright's American locution, it was American democracy needing a new architecture.)

But things were never so simple, in part because you can never measure a time solely by what its avant-garde is thinking and doing. Modernism created extraordinary works, but it did not have sole possession of the early twentieth century. As we look back at the architecture that was produced in the years before

Cass Gilbert, Woolworth Building, New York

World War I, there is no greater representation of that time than, say, Carrère and Hastings's New York Public Library, or Warren and Wetmore's Grand Central Terminal, or James Gamble Rogers's Memorial Quadrangle on the Yale campus, or Charles McKim's Pennsylvania Station, or Cass Gilbert's Woolworth Building. These are all traditional buildings—some Gothic, some classical, but every one of them heavily reliant on historical style rather the modernist architecture that, by the 1910s, was already becoming a part of the culture. And yet today we think of them as being totally representative of their time, and they are. James Gamble Rogers's Gothic-style buildings at Yale were no more truly of the Middle Ages than Charles McKim's Pennsylvania Station was truly of the Roman period. They were buildings of the early twentieth century, and they represent that time to us now as well and as fully as any work of modernism.

Today we realize that modernism did not have sole possession of the right to define the time, as it claimed. That is really the point, that the defining architecture of the early twentieth century was not only that which was dramatically and powerfully different; that period could also be defined, as can ours, by architecture that is heavily and unambiguously reliant on historical style. If buildings like the great structures I mentioned a moment ago truly didn't represent their time, they would not have the iconic status that they do for us today. We would think of them, if we thought of them at all, as irrelevant throwbacks, as leftovers produced by recalcitrant architects who didn't get with the program, as buildings that hardly mattered now.

Of course that isn't the case. Buildings like the Woolworth

Building and Grand Central Terminal and Harkness Tower at Yale—and thousands more like them—*are* their time, and they still define it, with brilliance and power. The moralistic argument—that the only way to be true to one's time is to create something completely new and different from what has come before—is one of those axioms that sound impressive when you first hear them but turn out not to mean very much once you try to probe them deeply.

The belief that there was indeed a style for the time, and that it was inherently superior to the reuse of a style from a previous time, affected the reception that one of the greatest museum buildings of the twentieth century, the National Gallery of Art in Washington, by John Russell Pope, received when it opened in 1941. By then, the building of the Museum of Modern Art in Midtown Manhattan was already two years old. While modern architecture had not yet become the accepted standard for public buildings, by 1941 it was far beyond seeming strange, radical, and new. The decision to design the National Gallery in a classical style struck many people as consciously and deliberately rearguard, which indeed it was. Yet Pope's building is one of the most inviting, elegant, and functional art museums ever built, with sumptuous galleries arrayed in a straight line extending from either side of a grand marble rotunda. The building is huge, but its organization is clear and straightforward; unlike in most traditional art museums, it is impossible to get lost in the National Gallery. The galleries are larger than the rooms in a house, but not so big that they feel institutional, and every one of them is lit by natural light from above. The detailing is cool and precise,

John Russell Pope, exterior view, National Gallery of Art, Washington, D.C.

almost severe; the opulence is always tempered by reserve. Pope had the rare ability to design buildings that were large and grand but not overbearing; for all its formality and dignity, nothing about this building is pompous. You sense that Pope was using classicism as a source of dignity and that he was distilling it down to its essence. That is the real brilliance of the National Gallery: it is classicism distilled to a pure, powerful, and spare, and everything within it is designed to show the paintings to their best advantage.

In this sense it worked far better than many modern museums, a fact that was not seen, or at least not acknowledged, by the critics of the building, who dismissed it as tired and fuddy-duddy, a sign that the United States could look only backward in its public buildings, not forward. The designers of the National Gallery were indeed looking backward, but it mattered less than people thought, since the quality of the building was so extraordinary that it transcended style. The building was so strong in its architectural fundamentals—in its scale, in its materials, in its organization, in its details, and above all in how it served the needs of both the paintings in the collection and the people who came to see them—that the rear-guard nature of its classical garb could be said, in one sense, to have been almost beside the point.

Indeed, the Pope building is considerably more honest, in some ways, than its modern addition, the East Building of the National Gallery by I. M. Pei, completed in 1978. Pei's building is a powerful composition of diagonals, built out of the same Tennessee marble as the original National Gallery beside it, but almost nothing else is the same about the two buildings. The sharp diagonals say "modern" as clearly as Pope's columns said "classical"; they are every bit as powerful an architectural signal. But as for honesty and clarity, those supposed modernist virtues, they are largely absent in the Pei building, which becomes somewhat confusing to understand and navigate your way around once you get past its spectacular, skylit atrium. The atrium is a splendid civic space, but the galleries, instead of flowing majestically out of the central space as they do from Pope's rotunda, are largely huge loft spaces set in differing points around the building, and which need to be designed anew for each installation. There is no sense that the specific demands of displaying art were the driving force in determining the design, as they were for John Russell Pope. So which is more "functional"—the classical portion of the National Gallery or the modernist one?

Modernist theorists have tried to make the argument that to

I. M. Pei, exterior view, National Gallery of Art East Building,
Washington, D.C.

build in the latest style is to be true to one's time, and to build in
a style that resembles the architecture of the past is false—a
betrayal of one's time, you could almost say. But it has never
been that simple. Styles are languages, and languages continue to
change and evolve. English today is different from the language
of Shakespeare's time or even George Bernard Shaw's. The greatest architects who have worked in past styles, architects from
Thomas Jefferson to Sir Edwin Lutyens to Léon Krier and Jaquelin Robertson, see historical architecture as a chance to say new
things in an existing language, not merely to copy what has been
said before.

If I can make the issue even more complicated, by the time
the East Building went up in the late 1970s, modernism was

beginning to take on a different connotation in our culture, since it was coming itself to be a part of history. Since many of the most important modern buildings had been constructed in the 1920s or before, by the 1970s many of the buildings by the early modern masters such as Wright and Le Corbusier and Mies van der Rohe were more than half a century old. Modernism was a mature, established style, not quite as established as the classicism John Russell Pope had used, but after a generation of modernist corporate headquarters and office towers and public buildings, you could hardly call it the daring and radical style it once had been. (You could almost say that by 1978, Pei was in some ways being just as conservative as Pope.)

And since then, modernism has receded still farther into history. In the twenty-first century, when an architect like Robert A. M. Stern designs a mansion in the Georgian style or a country house in the manner of the nineteenth-century Shingle Style, does it mean something all that different from what it means when an architect like Charles Gwathmey chooses to create a large and sumptuous modernist house inspired by the work of Le Corbusier? The architects themselves may feel it is quite different, but I'm not sure that we need to agree with them. Each architect is inspired by something he has admired from the past to design something new in the present that does not precisely resemble anything that has been built before. Each is being inventive within a particular design vocabulary, and the fact that the Georgian mansion traces its ancestry back to one century and the modernist villa to another may not mean all that much to us, in the end. Today, both look back. And our time, like every other, gets to reinterpret the historical languages of architecture on its own terms.

But since the era does matter, what is it, then, that defines a time? Why is Delano and Aldrich's Knickerbocker Club on Fifth Avenue in New York, which is one of the most beautiful Georgian-style buildings ever created, still a building of the twentieth century and not of the eighteenth, which its architects clearly wanted it to resemble? What makes the sprawling Houses of Parliament a Gothic building of the nineteenth century and not one of the sixteenth? Some of the answer lies in the technology of building materials—large buildings of the twentieth century are almost always built on steel or reinforced concrete skeletons, whatever stylistic surface is applied to them. The Gothic elements in Cass Gilbert's Woolworth Building, finished in 1913, were so striking that a prominent rector dubbed the tower "The Cathedral of Commerce." But underneath all of Gilbert's terra-cotta Gothic ornament was a fully modern skyscraper. The same can be said of McKim, Mead and White's old building for Tiffany and Company on Fifth Avenue in New York, of 1906, which was inspired by the Palazzo Grimani in Venice. But the building hardly resembled a sixteenth-century Venetian palace on the inside. Like the new Shingle Style house that is designed to look like a mansion from 1902 but has a huge, eat-in family kitchen and a media room, the interior almost always reveals the time.

But there is something else, more subtle perhaps, that marks buildings like these as being of the twentieth century and reveals them as contemporaries of the modernist architecture that was created in the hope of making them go away. Most late-nineteenth- and early-twentieth-century buildings in historical styles have a certain softness and picturesqueness about them, as if their architects were interested in visual ease above all. They lack the toughness of the truly new. They are stage sets—wonderful stage sets to be sure, but rarely do they have the ability to do more than give us visual pleasure. In those years it was the modern buildings that had the awkward brilliance of the new.

What I mean to say is that there really is a zeitgeist, a spirit of the time; it is just not so narrow as Le Corbusier or Walter Gropius would have had us believe, and not so limited to the cutting edge. Every age has its sensibility, and architecture inevitably both reflects and reveals it: the grandiose classical buildings of the City Beautiful movement at the end of the nineteenth century went hand in hand with the growing imperial ambitions of the United States, just as the acceptance of modernist architecture by the corporate world after World War II was a natural expression of the widely held belief that a new postwar era was beginning, with America's economic growth at its center. Within all of these large trends, of course, are smaller, briefer fashions. People tend to want buildings that look like other buildings, just so long as they are not identical, just as they like to dress almost, but not quite, the way other people dress. When an architect produces an appealing variation on a common style, it often spreads as any fashion does.

I have come to believe that time means at least as much as place, and often more, in determining what kind of architecture gets built almost anywhere that is not cut off from other places.

Gothic architecture reached its most glorious heights in France, but it was hardly limited to France, just as the return to classicism represented by the Renaissance, for all we think of it as being centered in Italy, manifested itself in much of Europe. In our own time, think of how the commercial districts of almost every American city in the late nineteenth century contained buildings of dark stone or red brick in vaguely Romanesque style, with elaborate arches and cornices—buildings that owed a debt to the great architecture of both Henry Hobson Richardson and Frank Furness and could be found in Boston and Dallas and Denver and Minneapolis and New York and San Francisco. The same thing could be said of skyscraper designs from the 1920s or suburban colonial-style villas or postwar glass office towers. In each case, the time marks the buildings far more than the place. (We might say the same about the form of cities. San Francisco and Los Angeles are both in California, but they could not be more different, less because of their geography than because San Francisco is a city of the nineteenth century and Los Angeles a city of the twentieth.)

Technology also plays an enormous role in determining the architecture of an era. People have always built what technology allowed them to build, whether it was the columns of Greek architecture, the arches and viaducts of Roman architecture, the flying buttresses that supported Gothic cathedrals, the high domes of the Renaissance, or the steel frames that made the first skyscrapers possible. The Metropolitan Life Tower in New York, which was the tallest building in the world from its completion in 1909 until the Woolworth Building was finished four years later, is a close copy of the campanile of St. Mark's in Venice. But it is vastly bigger, and it is not hard to tell that there is a modern skyscraper underneath that fancy garb, just as there is under the Gothic tracery of the Woolworth Building. Pushing technology to the limits defines the swooping concrete forms Eero Saarinen designed in the late 1950s, such as the TWA Terminal at Kennedy Airport and the Ingalls Hockey Rink at Yale, both of which seem primitive beside the more flamboyant and sculptural buildings produced some forty years later by Frank Gehry. Gehry buildings like the Guggenheim Museum Bilbao or the Walt Disney Concert Hall in Los Angeles, which could not have been produced without the aid of computers, carry the invention of form far beyond what Saarinen and others could do a generation ago. More recently still, the computer has given us a whole genre of buildings known as "blob architecture," with strange, amoeba-like shapes that clearly reflect the computerized origin of their designs. Not all architecture reflects technology in its form, as we have seen. But almost all of it takes advantage of it in its innards. As technology advances, architecture responds to the potential it offers, as it has since the beginning of building.

Buildings relate to the issue of time in another way, and that is in how, as Lewis Mumford said, they make time itself visible. A city resonates with the layers of time it reveals through its buildings. There is something off-putting about a place that is entirely new. It may excite you for a moment, but you rapidly sense the absence of history. There is novelty to Las Vegas or to the Pudong section of Shanghai, but it wears off quickly, since it all feels like a surface. A city—or a town or a village—should feel as if it began long before you and will go on long after you. It should have a patina. It should have gravitas, which older buildings confer naturally, especially if they are good ones. Older buildings give a place an anchor in time. It should almost go without saying that preserving old buildings is the right thing to do.

But how many of them should we be saving, and where? If preservation of older architecture is the goal, how does this not conflict with the fact that real places are not static? Colonial Williamsburg is one thing, but real cities are not museums. They grow and change. They have to grow and change; if they do not, they are dead. Period. If a city preserves everything, no matter how good its architecture is, keeping new life flowing through its veins becomes much more difficult, all the more because Americans have a tendency to preserve important buildings as if they were fragile hothouse orchids, wanting them to look pristine and perfect and show no sign of the passage of time. European cities have often done better than American ones at this, in part because Europeans are much more relaxed about their old buildings—they do have so many of them, after all—and they are less inclined to think of them as artifacts that must be handled with kid gloves. The conversion of the spectacular Gare d'Orsay in Paris into the Louvre's wing for nineteenth-century art and the creation of the Tate Modern out of a vast power station on the South Bank in London may not have resulted in the most perfect of museums, but both projects make the point that great older buildings can take some pushing and pulling and can in fact be enriched by participating in a dialogue between their own time and ours. Italy is full of seventeenth- and eighteenth-century buildings that have been given spectacular modern interiors. The Italians seem to feel that this kind of thing is precisely what keeps their old buildings alive.

I once heard a very simple but wonderfully poetic phrase, "the ever continuing past," and that says it perfectly, since it suggests a past that is not only visible but has an ongoing life that in some meaningful way connects with the present: a living past, you might say. Here, there may be the beginning, at least conceptually, of a way of resolving the conflict between preservation and real life. In a place with an ever continuing past, the past is not something sealed off to look at, and then we go back to the rest of our lives. It is a place in which the past helps to define the present, and in doing so it continues to evolve. The meaning of the past changes as each age uses it differently, views it differently, interprets it differently. In an ever continuing past, old buildings have a meaningful use in the present. It may be very different from its original use—a printing plant may become condominiums, or a factory may be turned into an office, or a courthouse may become a library. Sometimes this brings significant changes to a building's appearance (and what constitutes sensitive change to original architecture is a whole subject in itself), but often buildings will end up looking almost as they did originally, with everything required to meet twenty-first-century needs neatly hidden from view. The most important thing is that in the course of preserving a building it is not disconnected from the present but intimately tied to it.

Of course none of this is easy. And if a historic building stands in the way of a new one, who is to judge which has the right to occupy the land? Is it entirely up to the property owner? Or is there some public interest to be served in limiting the property owner's rights to tear a building down? Sir John Summerson foresaw the dilemma of historic preservation in the modern world in 1947 in an essay entitled "The Past in the Future," originally a lecture that he revised to become a chapter in his classic work on architecture, *Heavenly Mansions.* Summerson began by noting that the products of most cultural efforts, such as art and literature, are easy to preserve. He went on: "But old buildings are different. Like divorced wives, they cost money to maintain. They are often dreadfully in the way. And the protection of one may exact as much sacrifice from the community as the preservation of a thousand pictures, books or musical scores. In their case only, we are brought face to face with decisions on values. And these values are complicated."

Summerson went on to list the various categories in which he believed preservation could be justified, ranging from "the building which is a work of art" to "the building which . . . possesses in a pronounced form the characteristic virtues of the school of design which produced it." His last category was particularly telling: "The building whose only virtue is that in a bleak tract of modernity, it alone gives depth in time."

In New York, the pressures of growth and change have been intense for more than two hundred years, and they have made grappling with the decisions on values to which Summerson refers something of a local sport. In 1965, after the city lost McKim, Mead and White's incomparable Pennsylvania Station,

McKim, Mead and White, Pennsylvania Station, New York

New York established an official Landmarks Preservation Commission charged with preserving the city's important architecture. The legal basis for it was in the police power of the city government; in other words, in the rationale that this was a public benefit that the city had the right to enforce. The law said that preserving the city's most important buildings was "a public necessity . . . required in the interest of the health, prosperity, safety and welfare of the people," and pointed out the benefits to the economy as well as to civic pride.

The law prevents the commission from designating any building that is less than thirty years old, a reasonable enough way of letting the cycles of taste that I discussed at the beginning of this chapter play out. Beyond that, the commission uses criteria not unlike Summerson's to make its decisions. By its fortieth anniversary in 2005, it had designated 1,120 individual landmarks, 104 interior landmarks, and nine scenic landmarks. It has also gone beyond Summerson to establish eighty-three historic districts, of which the best known are such neighborhoods as Greenwich Village, Brooklyn Heights, SoHo with its extraordinary inventory of cast-iron buildings, and the Upper East Side; together the districts protect twenty-three thousand buildings. What is best about these districts is that they have reinforced the ongoing life of the city. They are not attempts to pretend that time is frozen. "It is impossible to preserve the 'character' of a place when the life in that place has completely changed," Sir John Summerson wrote. He is right, of course. But the strength of the best historic districts is that they do not attempt to make a false past, in the manner of Disneyland, but to use the past to shelter a vibrant present.

New York being what it is, the pressures to build new have not ceased, nor should they. The intention of the preservation effort was to save the most important architecture and establish a sense of balance between new and old, something that the city once seemed able to achieve naturally but by the second half of the twentieth century no longer could—in large part, I think, because the commercial architecture of New York (and so many other cities) in the postwar years was so mediocre as to make almost anything else look better than what was planned to replace it. At Pennsylvania Station, real estate developers added insult to injury by replacing one of the greatest public buildings in American history with a particularly mediocre box of an office

Charles Luckman, Madison Square Garden, New York

building and an ugly round drum containing a new Madison Square Garden. There, modernism had been misread, perhaps willfully, by people who used its principles of simplicity and functionalism not as a route to aesthetic purity but simply as an excuse for cheap, mean construction. This happened all over the city in those years, and it heightened the distrust of modern architecture and significantly increased the desire to save older parts of the city, raising the consciousness of the nascent historic preservation movement. It's worth remembering that the early years of historic preservation were born as much in dislike of modern architecture as in love of older architecture—in other words, as much out of fear of what would be built as out of love for what people were trying to preserve.

It was hard to blame people for preserving out of fear when the results were like Madison Square Garden. Once, certainly in the nineteenth century and for much of the twentieth, there was a sense that if something valued were lost from the cityscape, something equally valued, perhaps even more valued, would replace it. Central Park West when it was first developed in the 1880s had a mix of decent but not distinguished brownstones and residential hotels, very typical of what Lewis Mumford would call "the brown decades." One exception was at Sixty-second Street, where the Century Theatre, a distinguished Beaux-Arts building by Carrère and Hastings, architects of the New York Public Library, stood. Gradually over the 1920s and 1930s, these older buildings, or most of them, began to give way. The Century Theatre was replaced by the Century Apartments, one of the city's Art Deco treasures. The Majestic Hotel was replaced by the Majestic Apartments, the San Remo Hotel by the San Remo Apartments, the Beresford Hotel by the Beresford Apartments, all buildings of great distinction. In each case, one landmark was replaced by another. And sometimes the newer one was actually better.

So, too, across town, where the old Waldorf-Astoria Hotel by Henry Hardenbergh gave way to the Empire State Building, or on upper Fifth Avenue, where the Lenox Library by Richard Morris Hunt went down not for an apartment house but for a building that was actually smaller and lower, Carrère and Hastings's mansion for Henry Clay Frick, now the Frick Collection. We shouldn't forget the Plaza Hotel, also by Henry Hardenbergh, replacing a lesser, and fairly ordinary, earlier hotel of the same name, or the Bergdorf Goodman store on Fifth Avenue replacing

Carrère and Hastings, Century Theatre, New York

the Vanderbilt mansion, an even grander work by Richard Morris Hunt, or Rockefeller Center replacing blocks of mostly undistinguished brownstones and commercial buildings. The point is that change did not necessarily mean decline. The loss of familiar older buildings often brought with it the tradeoff of much better new ones.

A few stories from the early years of the landmarks commission make clear the extent to which attitudes about particular buildings change over time and how much the issue of preservation can affect the life of a city. The commission became involved in a critical battle over the future of one of the city's most important residential landmarks, the Villard Houses, another McKim,

Irwin Chanin, Century Apartments, New York

Mead and White masterpiece, this one on Madison Avenue right behind St. Patrick's Cathedral. A U-shaped cluster of brownstones from the 1880s inspired by the Palazzo della Cancelleria in Rome, the houses were occupied primarily by Random House, the publisher, which in 1967 announced its intention to move to a new office building, putting the landmark brownstones, to use the terminology of today's financial operators, "in play." The houses hadn't been residences for a very long time—the questions were first, whether they would survive at all, and second, in what form and for what purpose.

The houses were designated landmarks in 1968, the year after Random House announced its intention to move. Random

McKim, Mead and White, Villard Houses, New York

House owned its portion of the complex, and the Archdiocese of New York owned the rest. The fear that they would be demolished was widespread, and in 1974, the developer Harry Helmsley proposed a plan to purchase the houses and put up a hotel and office space adjacent to them. After many different versions and endless negotiations, Helmsley finally built his Palace Hotel, and it looked—well, mediocre, but at least the houses were saved. The houses still look sad, nestled at the bottom of a banal slab of a tower, with their backs sliced off so the center section looks like no more than a stage set—but presumably it was better than nothing.

Around the same time, another landmarks question arose on

West Eleventh Street, one of the most cherished blocks of early-nineteenth-century brownstones in Manhattan. In 1970, one of the finest houses, at 18 West Eleventh, was owned by an advertising man named James Wilkerson, whose daughter, Cathlyn Wilkerson, was active in a radical political group called the Weathermen. She and some friends decided to make a bomb to use in political protests—it was thought that they intended to bomb buildings at Columbia University—while her family was away in the Caribbean; something went horribly wrong, and the bomb exploded. Three people were killed, and the house so severely damaged that the insurance company insisted that the wreckage be torn down.

The architect Hugh Hardy purchased the site the following year and designed a new townhouse that fit smoothly into the old townhouse row in some ways but in other ways made some striking departures from the historical precedent. "It is condescending and unpractical to assume we understand another time well enough to recreate it," Hardy said at the time. "The past is not a costume rack that we loot to suit our fancy."

Hardy preferred, instead, to acknowledge historical reality—to admit in the nature of his design that it was the 1970s, not the 1840s. "I had no wish to pretend that the nineteen seventies did not exist," he said. But he also wanted to connect, to relate, and to acknowledge that his building was a part of a larger whole, and his design skillfully balanced these two things, connection to context and newness.

Because the block was part of the Greenwich Village Historic District, the Landmarks Preservation Commission had

Hugh Hardy, Townhouse, 18 West Eleventh Street, New York

jurisdiction over anything new that was to be built there. And at a public hearing to review Hardy's design, there was widespread pressure from neighbors to re-create the house as it had been. "I cannot accept the thought of badly reproducing a house of 1844," Hardy said. "I have tried to knit the wall of the street back together, but with a structure suitable to ourselves."

Now that this house has been there since 1979—built ultimately not for Hardy's family but for some other people to whom he sold the lot and the design—it is hard to realize that it once inspired bitter controversy, but so it was. The landmarks commission was sharply divided and finally approved the house by a narrow margin, with some people feeling that by doing so, it was allowing a radical intervention into a sacred historic district and others worried that all the pressure to re-create historical buildings as if it were another century was going to turn historic districts into Disneyland.

At around the same time as this mini-tempest was brewing, a really big one was heating up in Midtown Manhattan, one that would become, in a way, the most important preservation battle of all. It involved Grand Central Terminal, and even though the outcome is no mystery—things ended up a lot better than at Pennsylvania Station—it is worth explaining just how this building was saved. The saga begins in 1954, when the New York Central Railroad, which in the 1950s had begun to treat its great train station as shabbily as the Pennsylvania was treating its monument, announced that it was considering tearing the building down for redevelopment. The architect I. M. Pei, who in those days worked for the development firm of Webb and Knapp, came up with one scheme, and an architectural firm called Fellheimer and Wagner, successors to Reed and Stem, the original architects, produced another. Pei's at least was a wild, futuristic, eighty-story tower that narrowed at the center, like a tapered waist; the building would have been tremendously exciting, though hardly worth losing Grand Central for. The other proposal was—well, let's just say it represented 1950s blandness, only more so.

The New York Central wasn't quite ready to pull the trigger, and neither project happened. In 1967, the Landmarks Preservation Commission, over the opposition of the railroad, designated the terminal a landmark. The idea of building came back the next year, this time in the form of a tower, to be designed by the celebrated Bauhaus architect Marcel Breuer, which would rise

Marcel Breuer, proposed tower for atop
Grand Central Terminal, New York

directly above the terminal. The controversy over this one made
Penn Station seem mild. The landmarks commission said no,
and Breuer came up with a second version, in which the supports
for the tower came down in front of the facade, effectively block-
ing it but saving the entire concourse inside, which the earlier
version did not do. In 1969 the commission said no to that one,
too, and the railroad and its development partner sued the city,

arguing both that denying a building permit constituted an unconstitutional taking of their property rights and that declaring the station a landmark placed an unfair burden on the New York Central as a property owner. They asked for eight million dollars in damages for each year the project was delayed.

The railroad won the suit in 1975. Immediately the preservation community, which was growing increasingly vocal, began to protest. Philip Johnson and Jacqueline Kennedy Onassis formed the Committee to Save Grand Central. Johnson said, "Europe has its cathedrals and we have Grand Central Station. Europe wouldn't put a tower on a cathedral."

The Appellate Division of the New York State Supreme Court overturned the decision ten months later, saying that economics "must be subordinated to the public weal." The case was appealed, and in 1978, it reached the United States Supreme Court, the first historic preservation case ever to come before the Court. This was the ultimate test of the validity and the constitutionality of the idea of declaring a building a landmark, something that had never before been tested in the Court. And it passed. By a vote of six to three, the Court ruled in favor of the landmarks commission, upholding the constitutionality of the New York landmarks law and confirming the idea that a community designating buildings for preservation was as legitimate a form of land-use regulation as zoning.

So if Pennsylvania Station was the martyr of preservation, Grand Central became its triumphant savior, and it stands today, fully restored, perhaps in better shape than it has ever been. The principle of historic preservation is now accepted in New York, so much so that the arguments often seem to be between preservation fundamentalists, who want to preserve almost everything, and those who take a more measured view. No longer is it simply a fight over the basic idea of saving older buildings.

Still, it is hard not to wonder what New York would be like if there had been a landmarks commission in the 1950s. Pennsylvania Station would almost surely have been saved, but would the Guggenheim Museum have been built? Probably not, if preservation fundamentalists had been in charge. If the landmarks commission had been around in the 1930s, I suspect it would have saved Carrère and Hastings's great Century Theatre on Central Park West, which would have enriched New York. But would it have been worth never having gotten Irwin Chanin's magnificent Century Apartments? All the way through the 1930s it was fair to assume that when a much-admired building in New York was demolished, it would be replaced by another building of great quality. By the 1950s and 1960s, that was no longer the case. When the old Metropolitan Opera House, one of New York's most beloved buildings, was torn down in 1966 to make way for a mediocre office tower, it seemed only to compound the insult of losing Pennsylvania Station. There was no longer any pretense of an architectural tradeoff.

A building lost is never regained. That is perhaps the strongest argument for proceeding cautiously and assuring that the difficult decisions about what to save are not made in response to the short cycles of taste and fashion. For years, the cast-iron buildings of SoHo were dismissed as tired relics; so were the heavy masonry buildings of the 1880s and 1890s. In the same way, much closer to our time, Art Deco buildings were disdained for years as nothing more than cheap exercises in commercialism. Now, of course, all of these periods are cherished. It is worth remembering this as we think about how time will treat what we build today.

7
buildings
and the
making
of place

I have always claimed that places are stronger than people, the fixed scene stronger than the transitory succession of events. This is the theoretical basis not of my architecture but of architecture itself.

ALDO ROSSI

The street is a room by agreement.

LOUIS KAHN

Architecture never exists in isolation. Every building has some connection to the buildings beside it, behind it, around the corner, or up the street, whether its architect intended it or not. And if there are no buildings near it, a building has a connection to its natural surroundings that may be just as telling. Le Corbusier's Villa Savoye, his remarkable modern house in the Parisian suburb of Poissy that was finished in 1929, was designed to stand alone in an open meadow, a machine in the garden. But it is not really alone, any more than an apartment building standing shoulder to shoulder with other buildings a few miles away on the Boulevard Montparnasse is alone. The Villa Savoye was designed to open to its landscape on all four sides, and its landscape was designed to be a setting for the building. Neither house nor landscape would look the same without the other. More to the point, neither would have taken the form it did in the first place without the other. If Le Corbusier had designed the Villa Savoye for another site, it would have been another building.

In the case of some buildings, like Fallingwater, Frank Lloyd Wright's extraordinary house designed to cantilever over a waterfall in rural Pennsylvania, the connection between architecture and surroundings is obvious and unshakeable. More often, however, it is not so easy to see how buildings are designed in response to their surroundings and how buildings join with what is around them to create a sense of place. But join they do, even if the surroundings do not serve as the prime inspiration for a design, as they did at Fallingwater. A white clapboard colonial-style house with black shutters facing a New England village green is different from a similar house that sits on an open meadow, which in turn is different from the same house when it is behind a white picket fence on a country lane. The architecture of the houses may be similar, but the context makes them different. Take that house away from rural New England and put it onto a street in southern California—yes, there are houses like that sprinkled among the Spanish Colonial houses of Los Angeles—and it looks different again, this time by a factor of ten, since nothing about the surroundings seems naturally to fit. In the first three instances, the white clapboard house is among similar buildings, in a place—a New England village or a farm just outside of one—that has an innate connection to it. In Los Angeles, it feels out of place, in part because you associate such houses with the East Coast, and you instinctively feel that this one is out of context. Then again, in some parts of Los Angeles, the context is so varied that a street can well look like an architectural smorgasbord, where nothing fits very well (or everything fits just fine, depending on your viewpoint in such matters).

When buildings are fairly similar to each other, they make better streets. But what does fairly similar mean? If buildings are too much the same, the result can be oppressively dull. We look to the street, in part, for visual stimulation, and that depends on a certain amount of variety. Think of a classic small-town American Main Street, where there is likely to be a mix of brick and stone buildings, one, two, and three stories high. Some may have some stone ornament or decorated cornices, and others are plain. Some are thirty feet wide, others forty or fifty. One shop front may have a large sign, another a blue awning, another an old neon sign. There may be an old limestone bank with Doric columns, and perhaps, if the town is big enough, an office building that rises to six or seven or eight stories. No two of the buildings are the same, but they work together, largely because they are all fairly similar in scale—which is to say size in relation to the human figure—and overall size; they use similar materials; and they share a sense of responsibility to the street. They face the street, and they are organized for the benefit of people on the street. When Louis Kahn called a street "a room by agreement," he meant that there is a kind of implicit consent among architects of buildings on a street, an understanding that although they may choose to design different kinds of buildings, they will work together and not show each other up. Like dancers, architects follow one another's lead and endeavor not to step on any toes.

But that leaves plenty of room for architectural expression. One of the best streets in New York is Central Park West, which is far better than the stretch of Fifth Avenue that faces it across Central Park. Central Park West contains buildings ranging from Henry Hardenbergh's Dakota Apartments of 1884 to Robert A. M. Stern's 15 Central Park West of 2008, as well as four iconic twin-towered apartment houses from the early 1930s: the

Central Park West, New York

Century and the Majestic by Irwin Chanin, the San Remo by Emery Roth, and the El Dorado by Roth and the firm of Margon and Holder. Every one of these buildings is different, and none of them is what you would call restrained. It is a long way, both chronologically and architecturally, from the dark German Renaissance Dakota to the limestone-clad 15 Central Park West, which was designed to echo the late Art Deco buildings of the 1930s. But these buildings fit together the same way the ones in that hypothetical Main Street do, and for the same reason. For more than a hundred years, their architects honored the unspoken agreement to work together, to line their buildings up with each other and to work in a consistent scale and with materials that are compatible. The result is a boulevard that is both dignified and visually engaging. It is worth contrasting with Park

Avenue across town, where nearly identical apartment houses line both sides of the street for more than a mile and a half: there is coherence, but to a fault. Disorder has been kept so much at bay that the result is boring. Dignity is more appealing when it is combined with visual energy.

That helps explain why Paris, much of which is made up of essentially one building type, the eight-story stone apartment block, works so well: not merely because the buildings are similar —as Park Avenue shows, that is not always enough—but because they have so much visual energy in themselves. Moldings and cornices and balconies and grandly scaled windows and door-ways bring variety and texture to every one of those limestone facades on the wide Parisian boulevards, and they give your eye a degree of sensual pleasure. The average Parisian building has both lushness and solidity. Consistency here is perfectly balanced with variety. You feel a pattern—you know when you look at one of those apartment buildings that this is a type reproduced all over the city—but the idea of repetition never seems to take precedence over the visual pleasure that any one slice of the streetscape brings.

That is true to a certain extent in many European cities, though rarely quite as much as in Paris. In the western parts of London, in such neighborhoods as Knightsbridge and Kensing-ton, there are blocks and blocks of red brick Victorian houses that function in the same way as the white-painted townhouses of Belgravia do. (In Belgravia, there is almost too much consistency. It's the surprising richness of the off-white townhouses, which look almost as if they were made of frozen cream, that keeps your eye engaged.) The idea of rows of identical townhouses arranged in terraces or, better still, crescents, is particularly English. Two architects, a father and son both named John Wood, created a pair of extraordinary urban ensembles in Bath, the Circus and the Royal Crescent, in which town houses join together to create urban compositions that can only be called monumental. (The Royal Crescent is one of the most stunning urban vistas in the world.) And in London, John Nash's great ensembles at Regent's Park, including Regent's Park Crescent and Cumberland Terrace, as well as Carlton Terrace in St. James's, do much the same thing: individual row houses are put together into a combination that reads as a single work of architecture—vast, elegant, and urbane.

In the work of both Nash and the Woods, the individual houses are like members of a chorus line. They are supposed to look identical, and their moves are all calculated in terms of their effect on the whole. And like any chorus line, these work only because the director knew what he was doing. In lesser hands, the result would be confusion or boredom. But both Nash and the Woods also understood precisely how to balance texture with uniformity. The houses may look the same, but each member of this chorus line is attractive on its own. Like the Paris apartment houses—or, more to the point, like the Place Vendôme or the Place des Vosges in Paris, where identical structures surround a square—each building on its own conveys a sense of richness and sensuality. And their scale is comfortable and inviting. The Royal Crescent in Bath may be monumental, but its monumentality is made up of small parts that all feel accessible.

There are plenty of other models for an urban street beside the

John Wood the Younger, Royal Crescent, Bath, England

chorus line, and usually streets require more variety than these crescents, terraces, and circles possess. But they do demonstrate as powerfully as we could imagine an essential notion of urban design, which is that the whole is more than the sum of its parts. I will go further and say that this is the single most important principle of urban architecture: the whole is more than the sum of its parts. That doesn't mean that the parts need be the same or that they need to be as subjugated to the whole as in the work of the Woods and Nash. But it does mean that for a city to work, architects needs to feel as if they are designing a section of a much larger composition, a composition that began long before them and will continue long after them, and that however different their work may be from what adjoins it, they cannot design as if the other buildings were not there.

Planners and urban designers have tried for more than a century, without total success, to create formulas to assure that streets are attractive places to be. Camillo Sitte, the Viennese architect whose 1889 book *City Planning according to Its Artistic Principles* is in many ways the beginning of the field of urban design, argued against long, straight streets, which he thought were dull, and grandiose roundabouts like the Place d'Étoile in Paris, which he felt were impossible to cross. Sitte liked open plazas, situated irregularly, which he referred to as a city's "rooms." He felt a particular attraction to the medieval city, with its winding streets and changing vistas. His orientation was clearly to the pedestrian and to the notion of the city as an inviting rather than an intimidating environment.

I have a particular fondness for Trystan Edwards, an architect and theorist (though we stretch the latter term to call him that) who followed in Sitte's wake in 1924 with a book called *Good and Bad Manners in Architecture*. To Edwards, urban design and architecture were simply a matter of etiquette: as a person should respect one's neighbors, so should a building. Buildings, Edwards says, should show deference to one another. He praises traditional towns in which the hierarchy is clear: public and religious buildings are the most prominent, then shops, offices, and houses. "Civic order, social stability, and a fine, conservative temper are expressed by such an arrangement," Edwards wrote. "This precious standard of values, however, cannot be maintained when there is manifested a strong tendency for each building to display a spirit of selfishness, a profound disregard of its neighbors and of the city of which it forms a part." He goes on, not surprisingly, to denounce skyscrapers as the ultimate manifestation of the commercialism that disturbs him. "When we consider the general consequences of this too vigorous self-assertion on the part of individual shops it will be clear that such an architectural policy would be disastrous to the appearance of our streets," Edwards wrote.

Edwards's priggishness is amusing—in a chapter entitled "The Bugbear of Monotony," he has a section called "The Rude Gable"—and yet he was on to something. He knew that blocks of identical buildings are dull and also that fussiness and overdecoration is an unsatisfying response to the need for variety. (Another section is called "The Vice of Prettiness.") Underneath his pretense and his reactionary taste is a genuine understanding of the principles that make some city streets appealing and others not.

What Edwards understood is that cities have two types of buildings: background buildings and foreground buildings, and that they are different. They have different missions in the city, different meanings, and hence different architecture. A street or a neighborhood composed of too many foreground buildings will be a cacophonous mess, even if the buildings themselves are well designed. But a street with no foreground buildings at all will be a hopeless bore. Think, for example, of some of the blocks in London that are not special groupings of houses by John Nash or the like but are just long, long rows of identical brick houses. They are oppressively dull.

Foreground buildings do not have to resemble their neighbors, and often they are better if they don't. Frank Gehry's Guggenheim Museum Bilbao is a superb work of contextual architecture, not because it looks like anything around it—it is a highly sculptural object of titanium sitting amid old buildings of masonry—but because Gehry designed it with the neighboring buildings always in mind. It opens up magnificently to the river on one side, but when you see it from the other side, looking down one of the old city streets, there is an even more powerful view. The museum is a punctuation mark at the end of the vista, and it makes the city into a frame for its action. None of this is happy accident; Gehry paid as much attention to the surroundings of the Guggenheim in Bilbao as John Nash did to his surroundings in London. Gehry wanted his building to stand out—it was created specifically to stand out, to be a foreground building—but his way of standing out came not from indifference to what was around him but from a deep understanding of what was there and how a different kind of building might play off against it.

If I have learned anything about what makes a city feel comfortable as a work of design, it is that streets matter more than buildings. That may seem like an odd thing for an architecture critic to say, but urban delight is not the same thing as architectural pleasure, and good buildings are no guarantee of it. Some of the most appealing times I have had in cities around the world have been walks along streets that have no significant buildings at all: Madison Avenue in New York, the Strøtget in Copenhagen, Rue Jacob in Paris. Each of these streets has a sense of activity, pedestrian scale, and enough variety to keep

Frank Gehry, Guggenheim Museum Bilbao, Spain

your eye engaged, all the time. Monumental architecture would almost get in the way.

A city is much more than an assemblage of streets, however, and it is worth stepping back a bit farther to say something about the city at this moment in history, not only as a work of design but in a broader way, as a figment of our culture. How much do cities mean in an age of cyberspace, and how much does sense of place—one thing we expect buildings will help to give—matter? For all that our culture today celebrates architecture, even wallows in it, with spectacular buildings by famous architects increasingly the norm in large, medium, and small cities around the world, I am not sure that we any longer have the ability to create in a city as strong a sense of place as we once did. Paradoxically, the explosion of exciting architecture—what some people call "the Bilbao effect"—has not done much to counter the trend for cities to become more and more like other cities, and the sense of any place as special, rare, even unique, is fast disappearing. As J. B. Jackson, the great landscape historian, wrote in 1994, "Architecture in its oldest and most formal sense has ceased, at least in our newest landscapes, to symbolize hierarchy and permanence and sacredness and collective identity; and so far the road or highway has not taken over these roles."

What the road and highway began to do in recent generations, and what digital technology is doing now, is make places more and more the same. "The road generates its own patterns of movement and settlement and work without so far producing its own kind of landscape beauty or its own sense of place," Jackson wrote. "That is why it can be said that a landscape tradition a thousand years old in our Western world is yielding to a fluid organization of space that we as yet do not entirely understand."

Jackson's words are even truer for the age of cyberspace. This is not the place to delve fully into the homogenization of culture. But it is impossible to think about the meaning of architecture in our time without this fact, for its impact on architecture is tremendous. In an age in which American architects design skyscrapers for Singapore and Shanghai, when Swiss architects design museums in San Francisco and stadiums in Beijing, when McDonald's restaurants are to be found in Tokyo and Paris, when expressways create a similar automobile landscape almost everywhere, and an age in which suburban sprawl has made the outskirts of London look not so different from the outskirts of Dallas—is the very concept of sense of place now a frivolous luxury? If every city is truly going to look more and more like every other city, and every suburban node more and more like every other suburban node, then what is the point of special architectural expression at all?

Never mind that what is increasingly becoming an international form of architecture is fundamentally American and automobile-oriented. There is little pleasure in the cultural hegemony that this represents, particularly since the forces of sameness are affecting regions within the United States as much as around the world—Boston begins to look more and more like Atlanta, Denver like Houston, Charlotte like Cincinnati. And these cities' suburban rings are even more generic, products of time rather than of place. A suburban office park in Bethesda,

Maryland, is no different from a suburban office park in Portland, Oregon; there is nothing, not even the stores within, to distinguish a mall in Pittsfield, Massachusetts, from a mall in Fresno, California.

Architecture has always reflected its time, and must do so. But it has traditionally emerged from a sense of place as well as of time, reflecting the materials, the needs, the particular sensibilities and choices of individual cities and communities. Now, however, "sense of place" as a value has come to feel antiquated, almost quaint, as we travel rapidly from city to city, moving all the way across the world in a matter of hours, and more often than not we do not actually move at all, but communicate electronically in an instant. Even if we do not actually travel we are less rooted in a single place. Cities are way stations, not full and complete exemplars of our particular worlds. We pass through them, sometimes physically, sometimes only electronically, but either way, the connection is brief and tenuous.

The meaning of community, and hence the meaning of architecture, must change in such a world. We socialize online as much as in person, we speak in an instant via cellular telephone to people anywhere in the world, and human encounters shaped by their physical setting are increasingly rare. Physical surroundings do not matter in cyberspace—to protect us, and our computers, from the weather is the most important contribution architecture makes to conversation in cyberspace. It does not create a backdrop for conversation, and hence affect it in myriad subtle ways, as it does in "real" human encounters; it becomes invisible. Architecture is no longer a stage set for human drama. While it's true that webcams and video chats by computer change this somewhat by providing at least a visual backdrop, that is hardly the same as a setting. It is still hard not to feel that in cyberspace the role of architecture as a social enabler, as common ground, all but evaporates. Is architecture then irrelevant to the new world technology is making?

And yet, the technological revolution makes everything, in effect, a city. The random connections, the serendipitous meetings, that occur on the Internet, the replacement of linear order with the interlocking web of ties, broken and reformed and broken again a million times, the sense of accident and surprise—these are the very events that real physical cities have always provided and for which they have been valued. Random encounters are the city's greatest gift, and random encounters are cyberspace's stock-in-trade. It is not for nothing that commercial online services like to refer to their conversation areas with architectural analogies—the "town square," the "lobby," the "chat room"—and sometimes even show tiny computerized images of doors through which the curious may enter. The technological explosion is making the entire world a virtual city, a new city, the new marketplace of human encounters, which happens not to be defined by architectural form.

We are not entirely comfortable in this new city, however, and I think we are far from ready to give up on architecture. Buildings are not obsolete and won't become so. But they no longer define all of our public places and hence no longer provide the sole stage for public, and thus civic, experience. So it is inevitable that the meaning of architecture in our culture will continue to shift, as it has shifted during the previous technological advances of the past century. The automobile, the telephone, and television have affected how we use, and therefore design, both public and private space, and the computer will change things still more.

Whatever strength there may be in old cities, the traditional, dense city for which busy, active, people-filled streets are the measure of success is less and less something we can count on. For those situations in which we actually do come together physically and not virtually, we increasingly do so in places that represent a new model, something we might call a kind of para-urbanism or pseudo-urbanism, and it has at least as significant an impact on the evolving definition of the city as cyberspace does. This new urban model is characterized by valuing automobile access more than pedestrian accommodation and by a desire to combine the ease and convenience of the suburbs with the benefits of traditional cities: thus it has a variety of shops, restaurants, and public gathering places; facilities for the performing and visual arts; and the general level of excitement and stimulation associated with older, street-oriented cities. Sometimes these new kinds of places, these city-suburb hybrids, get built in the suburbs, sometimes they get built on the edges of cities, and sometimes they happen right inside the cities themselves.

Providing some measure of urban experience without encouraging the mixing of different kinds of people might be said to be the new urban paradigm: making the city safe for the middle class. If traditional cities have always demanded engagement, the new urban paradigm seems its absolute opposite. It sanctions disengagement even as it professes to celebrate the virtues of urbanity.

The new urban paradigm is less truly urban than a kind of blurring of the traditional differences between city and suburb. While numerous older cities now attempt to market themselves as lively, vibrant, culturally active environments, the purest examples of the new urban paradigm are surely the so-called edge cities that now exist on the outskirts of most large cities, combining shopping malls, hotels, office buildings, and occasionally housing at a density that is greater than traditional suburban density but significantly less than that of older core downtowns. Such places as City Post Oak in Houston, Tysons Corner outside Washington, Buckhead north of Atlanta, and Las Colinas outside Dallas mix high-rise buildings with shopping malls and hotels; gleaming and relatively new, they would seem to have every quality of cities except streets. Each of these places represents an attempt to take on the more benign characteristics once associated with larger cities without acquiring any other qualities of urban downtowns. The message is obvious: urbanity is attractive, so long as it can be rendered friendly and harmless.

This new urban paradigm began as a product of the automobile and flourishes now, of course, as a result of the explosion of technology. As I've already said, in an age of instant communication via the Internet, no one truly has to be anywhere. For many of us, where we choose to be is the result of other factors. People with the means to choose where they want to be often choose cities today not out of business necessity but for their excitement and pleasure. To some extent the future of all cities lies in their becoming at least a little bit like Venice or Amsterdam, places in which the tourist economy rules. The city can no longer lay claim to being the only place in which to do business, as it once could.

But the bulk of people cannot afford the choice of spending time in such settings, and the closest they get to real city life is in the place of this new urban paradigm, the edge city where urban values are increasingly suburban values. By suburban values of course I mean much more than matters of geography, and much more than accommodation to the automobile, though this is surely a part of it. Yet far more important are two much more subtle but ultimately far more profound aspects of suburban values: racial and economic segregation, and, going hand in hand with this, an acceptance, even an elevation, of the notion of private space. Indeed, the truly defining characteristic of this time might be said to be the privatization of the public realm, and it has come to affect our culture's very notions of urbanism.

Suburbs have traditionally valued private space—the single-family, detached house, the yard, even the automobile itself—over public space, which they have possessed in limited enough quantities under the best of circumstances. And most suburbs now have even less truly public space than they once did. Not only are malls taking the place of streets in the commercial life of many small towns, but the privatization of the public realm has advanced even more dramatically with the huge rise in the number of gated, guarded suburban communities, places in which residential streets are now technically private places rather than public ones. In literally thousands of such communities, entire neighborhoods become, in effect, one vast piece of private property. They exist to exclude, whereas traditional cities existed to include or at least had the effect of inclusion.

The rise of suburban values means much more than the growth of suburban sprawl, then. It has meant a change in the way public and private spaces work in both suburbs and cities. And it has meant that many cities, even ones that pride themselves on their energy and prosperity, have come to take on certain characteristics once associated mainly with the suburbs. Now in both city and suburb, expressions of urbanity, which we might define as the making of public places where people can come together for both commercial and civic purposes, increasingly occur in private, enclosed places: shopping malls, both urban and suburban; "festival marketplaces" that seem to straddle the urban-suburban models; atrium hotel lobbies, which in some cities have become virtual town squares; lobbies of multiplex cinemas, which often contain a dozen or more theaters and thus exist at significant civic scale; and office building gallerias, arcades, and lobbies. These are all private places, and even though the public uses them, they are not public as we have traditionally taken that term to mean.

There is another new model besides what I've called the new urban paradigm around these days, and it goes by the term New Urbanism. It arose in the 1980s in conscious reaction against the world of sprawl, mainly through the work of Andrés Duany and Elizabeth Plater-Zyberk, the Miami architects who designed Seaside, a new town on the coast of the Florida panhandle. In Seaside, architecture is strictly regulated through codes (which do not require traditional architecture per se, but tend to have the effect of encouraging it), and there is a carefully wrought plan of narrow, pedestrian-oriented streets. If Seaside can sometimes be faulted for seeming a bit too precious—not by accident was it used as the set for the film *The Truman Show*—it is exquisite and a genuine joy to walk through. It has at least some of the feeling of the village of Nantucket and the older sections of Charleston, and there are no better models for urban villages in the United States than those.

Since Duany and Plater-Zyberk designed Seaside it has been widely imitated, sometimes by them and sometimes by others, and it has become the touchstone of a broader movement to return to the kind of communities we built before the automobile blew cities apart. Some real estate developers have embraced New Urbanism in the same way that others have taken up edge cities, and the results have been uneven at best and all too often have the disingenuous, falsely sweet air of the theme park. You cannot make a valid place only out of yearning or out of trying to market nostalgia. But underneath it all there is a recognition that we need to regain the things that matter in the making of places: pedestrian scale; a close connection between living places and places to shop and, ideally, places to work; architecture that reinforces sense of place rather than gets in the way of it. At its best, the New Urbanism is not so much new as true—a dollop of bona fide urbanism for a culture that has all too often forgotten that architecture is a building block for streets and communities.

If you believe, as I do, that one of the greatest gifts architecture can give you is to go beyond the experience of a single building, however glorious that may be, and see what can happen when buildings come together to make a place, then the urban impulse, the idea of the city, and the idea of architecture are inseparable. Architecture is the making of place and the making of memory, and the role of the city is deeply intertwined with this pursuit. Our memories come from places at least as much as from buildings, and when buildings combine well to make places, whether it is the civic buildings surrounding a football field in Nutley, New Jersey, or the monuments of Rome, they resonate even more deeply than they do on their own. Good streets may indeed do more than great buildings to make cities livable, but no city has ever gotten far without serious architectural ambition as at least part of its makeup. Good buildings support us and serve as a civilizing backdrop to our daily lives; great buildings take us out of our daily lives and elevate us.

The role of any city, to put it as bluntly as possible, is to be a common place, to be common ground—to make a kind of common body of memory—and as such, to strengthen us and to stimulate us. "Now, the great function of the city is . . . to permit, indeed to encourage and incite the greatest possible number of meetings, encounters, challenges between all persons, classes and groups," wrote Lewis Mumford, "providing, as it were, a stage upon which the drama of social life may be enacted, with the actors taking their turns as spectators, and the spectators as actors." Mumford spoke of the city in terms not only of meetings and encounters but also of challenges: he knew that the city is difficult and did not attempt to pretend otherwise, to pretend that it is the easiest route. But he knew that in meeting challenge there is also a kind of satisfaction that cannot come from easy routes and that the challenge the city represents can, at its best, be ennobling.

Architecture, I will say again, is the making of place and the making of memory. The urban impulse is an impulse toward community—an impulse toward being together and toward accepting the idea that however different we may be, something unites us. But what do we do in an age when every force pushes us away from cities, pushes us apart rather than together? And how do we make valid, lasting memory when it becomes so easy not to see the familiar, when we take it for granted and no longer even notice it? As we move more and more into an age in which we do not automatically build cities, an age in which architectural experiences seem increasingly standardized and homogenized—and hence all the more susceptible to the dangers of familiarity—we have to think hard about how the experience of being together will come to pass and how architecture can express a sense of community, a sense of common ground, and still somehow be able to possess both vitality and valid meaning for our time.

Architecture represents the real, and that is ever more precious in an age of the virtual. Every piece of architecture is an opportunity for real experience. Some of the opportunities architecture offers us are banal, others are irritating, and some will not communicate at all. Some will give us comfort, which is of no small value. And some will be transcendent and will tell you, more eloquently than anyone can express in words, of that aspect of human aspiration that makes us want to connect to what has come before, to make of it something different and our own, and to speak to those who will follow us.

glossary

arch: The alternative to spanning an opening with a straight line, the arch—a combination of bricks or stones mounting upward in a curve—is exceptionally strong, because the curve directs the structural forces both downward and toward the center; an arch will "hold" in ways that a straight line will not. The Romans made great use of the arch in their monumental civic buildings and aqueducts; the invention of the *pointed arch* in the eleventh century was a key development in the evolution of *Gothic* architecture.

Art Deco: Originally referring only to architecture directly influenced by the Exposition des Arts Décoratifs in Paris in 1925, the term has come to describe almost any building from the 1920s and 1930s that attempts to give modernism a sleek, decorative flair, such as New York's Radio City Music Hall and Chrysler Building. *Art Moderne* and *Streamline Modern* are other terms that refer to what might be called jazz age modernism, modern architecture that is both more commercial and more zestful than the *International Style.*

atrium: The term for the inner courtyard of a traditional Roman house has been adopted in our time to refer to the large, covered multistory open space in the middle of a shopping mall, office complex, or hotel.

Baroque: The Baroque style began in sixteenth-century Italy as both an extension of Renaissance architecture and a reaction against it. Baroque architects used classical elements but combined them in ever more elaborate and complex ways, giving their buildings a sense of movement, depth, and emotional intensity. See also *Mannerism.*

Bauhaus: An extraordinary modernist design school that existed in Germany between 1919 and 1933, the Bauhaus brought together architects such as Walter Gropius, who designed its famous building in Dessau, Marcel Breuer, and Mies van der Rohe; artisans such as Anni Albers; and artists such as Josef Albers, Paul Klee, and Wassily Kandinsky. The Bauhaus sought to join art, craft, and technology, and its name has become synonymous with European architecture of the machine age.

Beaux-Arts: The École des Beaux-Arts in Paris was the most celebrated school of architecture in the world in the nineteenth century, and its students were taught to design buildings that were monumental, classical, highly sculptural, and generally symmetrical. The Beaux-Arts classicism was closely tied to the *City Beautiful movement* in the United States toward the end of the nineteenth century and yielded such major public buildings as the New York Public Library and Grand Central Terminal in New York. The high period of Beaux-Arts classicism in the United States is sometimes referred to as the *American Renaissance.*

classical: Pertaining to Greece and Rome, which in the case of architecture means not merely being ancient but referring to what has become the basic architectural language of the Western world. Classical architecture is based on Greek temples and Roman civil, military, and religious structures. It is known not only for specific elements such as *columns, entablatures,* and *pediments* but for an attitude that the architectural historian Sir John Summerson described as "the aim . . . to achieve a demonstrable harmony of parts."

colonial: Less an actual style than a catchall term that is often used to describe any American architecture dating from the period before the

Revolutionary War and later architecture designed to resemble it. Much colonial architecture is English in influence; some of it is Dutch, and some Spanish. In common usage, however, *colonial* connotes a house of wood or brick, often symmetrical, which might be called a much-simplified version of English Georgian architecture.

column: The vertical support in a classical building, typically made up of three parts: the base, or bottom; the shaft, or long midsection; and the capital, or top. There are five basic types, or orders, of classical columns: *Tuscan, Doric, Ionic, Corinthian,* and *Composite.* Each not only looks different, each sends distinct emotional signals. A selection of order, the architectural historian Sir John Summerson writes, "is a choice of mood." The term *column* is also used to describe a vertical structural support in any kind of building. A modern skyscraper, for example, is constructed on a steel or concrete frame consisting of vertical columns and horizontal beams. A line of columns supporting an *entablature* or a series of *arches* is called a *colonnade.*

Corinthian: The most ornate of the standard classical orders, a Corinthian column is marked by a capital that suggests acanthus leaves splaying outward. In some buildings the scrollwork top of an *Ionic* column is combined with the more flamboyant Corinthian to form what is called a *Composite* column.

curtain wall: The non-load-bearing, outer wall of a tall building, often of glass or metal, that is "hung" from the steel or concrete frame that supports the building.

dome: A spherical, oval, or polygonal roof, actually a type of *vault,* which is used to define space inside a building and to create a strong profile outside. Domes were first used by the Romans, who favored a low, circular shape, and became a key part of Renaissance and neoclassical architecture—so much so that the colloquial term for many Italian Renaissance cathedrals, such as the one in Florence, is the "Duomo." The small, round structure often placed atop a dome is called a *lantern.*

Doric: The Doric classical order is austere and powerful, its top consisting of a flat, simple slab above the shaft, the upper portion of which is usually marked by a plain band to distinguish it from the rest of the shaft, which is often fluted, or scalloped. In its Grecian form, the Doric column has no base at all.

eclectic: An architectural sensibility that encourages taking the best of many styles and is not bound to any single stance. The American architects of the first four decades of the twentieth century who eschewed modernism and moved freely back and forth between classical, Georgian, Tudor, Italian Renaissance, and Gothic styles were often referred to as "the eclectics," but the term can represent a philosophical attitude as much as describe a career.

elevation: A drawing of one side of the exterior of a building. Less frequently, the term is used to describe a drawing of an inside wall, often called an *interior elevation.* Together with the *plan* and the *section,* the elevation conveys the essential information about a design. Construction drawings are made up of a combination of elevations, plans, and sections.

entablature: The various elements that are supported by the column: the *architrave,* directly atop the column; the *frieze,* which often contains abstract ornament or sculpture; and the *cornice* at the top. The term *architrave* is often used to describe any molding around a door or window, as *cornice* is often used to describe the ornamental projection of the roof in any kind of building.

entasis: Columns are generally wider in diameter in the middle of the shaft than at the top or bottom, and the swelling, which corrects an optical illusion, is called *entasis.* Without the slightly convex line of entasis, a column would tend to appear concave.

facade: The front of a building, or the portion that is seen from the street.

Georgian: The architecture of eighteenth-century England, it is strongly neoclassical and particularly urbane. The Georgian style is among the most successful architectural languages ever created for establishing coherent groups of buildings along streets and urban squares.

Gothic: The medieval architectural style, which developed in the twelfth century and is marked by pointed arches, stained glass, and an overall sense of lightness in comparison with the architectural styles that preceded it. The Gothic cathedrals represented extraordinary structural innovation, including the invention of *flying buttresses,* external supports that enabled a cathedral's stone walls to resist the enormous pressure of the roof unsupported by vertical columns.

historical revivals: Most architecture has been based on other architecture, and often the predominant style of a time has been a reinterpretation of a previous period. The Renaissance was in a way a classical revival; in the eighteenth century, *Neoclassical* architecture would be a later form of classical revival. *Gothic revival* architecture was a powerful presence for much of the nineteenth century, as was *Romanesque revival.* Generally, historical revivals, unlike *eclecticism,* are characterized by a commitment to a style as ideologically correct.

International Style: The term, coined by Philip Johnson and Henry-Russell Hitchcock in their 1932 book and their later exhibition at the Museum of Modern Art, refers to the crisp, austere architecture of the early decades of the twentieth century, produced by mainly European architects such as Walter Gropius, Marcel Breuer, Le Corbusier, Mies van der Rohe, and J. J. P. Oud. Eventually the term would be extended to describe almost any architecture based on these early modern examples: glass office buildings of the 1960s, for example, are often referred to as being in the International Style.

Ionic: The Ionic classical order is marked by volutes, or coiled elements inserted atop the shaft, like a partially unrolled scroll. It is proper, reserved, and tightly wound, formal without being austere.

Italian Renaissance: The Renaissance, the rebirth of classicism after the Middle Ages, reached its highest expression in sixteenth-century Italy, where classical elements were rediscovered and combined in new and brilliant ways, codified by Donato Bramante, Andrea Palladio, Leon Battista Alberti, and Sebastiano Serlio, among others. There have been numerous revivals of Italian Renaissance architecture, particularly in the nineteenth century.

Mannerism: In part a transition from Italian Renaissance to the Baroque, Mannerism was a potent aesthetic, a kind of hyper-refinement of classical elements, often given a twist or interpreted in some unusual way to enhance their emotional intensity.

mass: The bulk of a building or its overall volume as a solid object.

modernism: The roots of the modern movement in architecture go back to the nineteenth century and to the first attempts to seek a clarity and a simplicity that would provide relief from dry and heavy-handed academicism: the *Arts and Crafts movement* in England, the *Secessionist movement* in Vienna, the *Art Nouveau movement* in France and the *Prairie Style* of Frank Lloyd Wright and his followers in the United States were all starting points of modernism. But what we tend to think of as "modern architecture" reached full flower in Europe in the first decades of the twentieth century, with the *Bauhaus* and the *International Style.* Today, *modernism* is used to refer both to this historical period and, less precisely, to architecture produced today.

New Brutalism: A reaction against the light, glass, and steel vocabulary of the *International Style* in the 1950s and 1960s, New Brutalism was characterized by harsh, bold concrete forms. Le Corbusier's late work is generally viewed as the inspiration for New Brutalism.

pilaster: A profile of a column, set flat against a building as a form of ornament rather than constructed as a freestanding, round element.

plan: The floor plan, or layout, of a building, it provides a kind of map of the various spaces within a building and helps to make clear the sequence of movement through a building. The plan is almost never an afterthought: indeed, sometimes an architect will create a plan before designing any other part of a building, and the plan will function as the primary organizing device and will be the basis of the fundamental architectural ideas.

portico: A columned porch or entry area to a building, based loosely on Greek temple form.

postmodernism: If *New Brutalism* was a search for a different way to be modern, postmodernism was an attempt, beginning in the 1970s and flourishing in the 1980s, to reject the indifference to history that marked orthodox modernism and to reintroduce many elements of historical architectural styles. Postmodernist architects at first were less inclined toward literal copying of historical style than toward reinterpretation of historical elements, often in the form of collage. Eventually the term began to be used loosely to describe almost any contemporary architecture that was not overtly modern, and it lost its original meaning.

Rococo: A variant emerging out of the Baroque, mainly in France and Germany, Rococo architecture was even more highly decorated, often with curving, scallop-shell motifs and pastel colors. Rococo generally substituted lavishness of decoration for the structural and spatial inventiveness of the great Italian Baroque.

Romanesque: Medieval, pre-Gothic architecture, heavier and more rounded than the Gothic. A major *Romanesque Revival* took place in the late nineteenth century, most notably in the work of the great American architect Henry Hobson Richardson; this style is sometimes called *Richardsonian Romanesque.*

scale: Scale is conceptual size, which is to say the size of elements in relation to the human figure and also to one another. To say that something is "out of scale" is not to say that it is large or small but that its size is disproportionate to other elements, including other buildings, or to the human figure.

Second Empire: An ornate, even grandiose, architectural style from the mid-nineteenth century marked by high mansard roofs, elaborate sculpture, and often a sense of multiple pavilions making up a monumental facade. Named for the reign of Napoleon III of France, the style left a major mark on American public works late in the nineteenth century in such buildings as the Philadelphia City Hall and the Old Executive Office Building next to the White House.

section: A drawing made by cutting an imaginary vertical slice through a building, showing the ceiling heights of each floor and the height of special spaces such as atriums. The section is the complement to the *plan,* and together the two convey essential information about the interior of a building.

Spanish Colonial: The red tile roofs, stucco walls, open colonnades, and pergolas of Spanish Colonial revival architecture have now become so ubiquitous as a residential and commercial style in most of the American West and Southwest that it is hard to remember that it did not emerge whole but grew out of a combination of Spanish elements from early missions and the distinct regional architecture created out of adobe for the pueblos of Arizona and New Mexico.

style: Perhaps the hardest term in architecture to define, as well as the most overused. *Style* can refer to a historical period, such as *Gothic* or *Renaissance* or *Georgian;* it can also be used to mean an attitude and approach to architecture that a particular period represents. Most buildings do not fit neatly into stylistic categories, which is why many architectural historians break the broad stylistic labels down into multiple subcategories. But that can be a process without end, in part because the best buildings often redefine style rather than respond to it. Architectural historial Sir John Summerson's observation regarding the rules of classicism might be applied to all architecture: "If the understanding of rule is one basic factor in the creation of great classical buildings the defiance of rule is the other."

Tuscan: The plainest of the classical orders, it is similar to the *Doric* but with a shaft that is not fluted. Simplicity in the Tuscan order comes across as blunt and direct rather than refined and austere.

vault: A roof or ceiling in an arched shape, made of stone, brick, or tile. A *barrel vault* is a simple semicircle; more complex vaults are made up of intersecting sections, which have greater strength and can span greater distances: *groin vaults,* or intersecting barrel vaults; *rib vaults,* which use Gothic pointed vaults instead of semicircles; and *fan vaults,* which are more elaborate ornamented versions of rib vaults.

vernacular: Any common, everyday language of building, either historical or contemporary: a Tuscan stone farmhouse might be described as representing one vernacular style, a roadside drive-in as another.

Victorian: Like colonial, less a style than an umbrella phrase, in this case covering *Victorian Gothic, Queen Anne, Stick Style,* and even *Shingle Style,* all styles that prevailed at various points during Queen Victoria's reign. Queen Anne and Stick Style houses were elaborate, multifaceted compositions, often containing multiple gables, turrets, porches, and chimneys. The Shingle Style toward the end of the nineteenth century represented a partial simplification and a movement toward more unified, flowing form that helped to pave the way for the expansive horizontal lines of Frank Lloyd Wright's *Prairie Style.*

a note on bibliography

The list of sources for this book could conceivably include every meaningful book I have ever read about architecture, just as the list of influences cited in the Acknowledgments could include every noteworthy building I have ever seen. Could does not mean should, however, and I have no more desire to create such endless lists than readers do to read them. I will spare us both the burden. It is important, however, to cite a number of books that have played a major role in shaping the viewpoint that I express in this book, as well as to note some essential reference books, and to say a few words about other books that have been written over the years with the intention, like this one, of helping people understand more about the architecture that they are looking at as they go about their daily lives.

As a college student, I first encountered several books and one article that continue to resonate with me now. Robert Venturi's *Complexity and Contradiction in Architecture* (1966) is the book that, more than any other, helped me understand that the purism of orthodox modernism was in many ways a Procrustean bed and that there was no reason that aesthetic experience in contemporary architecture could not also be rich and complex. Its ideal complement is Jane Jacobs's *The Death and Life of Great American Cities* (1961), which attacked the folly of modernist urban planning even more forcefully than Venturi criticized the aesthetics of modernist architecture; more than forty years after their publication, both books are as important, and as convincing, as ever. Herbert Gans, in *The Urban Villagers: Group and Class in the Life of Italian-Americans* (1962), makes the same case as Jane Jacobs about the failure of modernist planning in terms of American urban renewal but is written more as the sad story of Boston's failure than as a broad polemic. Charles Moore's great essay "You Have to Pay for the Public Life," first published in the Yale architectural journal *Perspecta* in 1965 and later reprinted in Moore's superb collection of the same title, edited by Kevin Keim (2001), was and remains the clearest articulation I have ever read of the value of the public realm.

And while I am looking back, it is important here to cite three books that I remember from even earlier than my college years that I know played a role in shaping my feelings about architecture: Richard Halliburton's *A Book of Marvels* (1937), not really a book about architecture but as earnest and stimulating an ode to the power of place as any boy growing up in the 1950s could possibly read; and then, a little later, two books that I received as gifts: *Eero Saarinen on His Work* (1962), compiled by Aline Saarinen, and *Masters of Modern Architecture* (1958), by John Peter, both large-format books that introduced me to many of the architects whose work I would later encounter. (In a world that has been overwhelmed by monographs, which these days seem to be produced by any architect who has completed more than three buildings, few have been as dignified or as elegantly produced as the Saarinen book. As for the Peter, now there are dozens of coffee-table surveys of contemporary architecture, most of them better and all of them more up-to-date.)

It was also as a student that I happened upon Trystan Edwards's *Good and Bad Manners in Architecture* (1924), quite by accident as I wandered through the stacks of Sterling Memorial Library at Yale. (How many chance encounters with books no longer happen in these days of libraries with closed stacks or no stacks at all?) I found Edwards's attempt to equate architecture with etiquette to be endearing, if precious, and it did get me thinking about the question of what urbanism really means.

I also came across *How to Judge Architecture* (1903), by the architect Russell Sturgis, perhaps the first attempt to create a basic introduction for lay readers with the goal of teaching them not just to appreciate architecture but to make up their own minds about it. Far more important to my own view of things are two incomparable books I have returned to again and again since I first encountered them: Sir John Summerson's remarkable collection of essays *Heavenly Mansions and Other Essays on Architecture* (1949) and Vincent Scully's *American Architecture and Urbanism* (1969). These are two very different kinds of books by two very different kinds of architectural historians, each a great scholar who proves again that solid history is not incompatible with masterful and highly personal writing. And both books stand as eloquent reminders of the importance of not treating architecture as if it existed in an aesthetic vacuum. So, too, with Scully's *Modern Architecture and Other Essays,* edited by Neil Levine (2003), an essential compendium of critical and historical writing; to read it is to experience the monumental arc of Scully's career, his changing preoccupations and his constant passion. Summerson's *The Unromantic Castle* (1990) is no less valued and proves again that Summerson was among our greatest essayists on architecture—as does another book that is itself a long essay, his slim but vital *The Classical Language of Architecture* (1966).

My copies of Geoffrey Scott's *The Architecture of Humanism: A Study in the History of Taste* (1924); Rudolf Arnheim's *The Dynamics of Architectural Form* (1977); Rudolph Wittkower's *Architectural Principles in the Age of Humanism* (1965); Gaston Bachelard's *The Poetics of Space* (1964); Karsten Harries's *The Ethical Function of Architecture* (1997); and the more recent *A Shout in the Street: An Excursion into the Modern City* (1990), by Peter Jukes (a remarkable "meditation" on the city that is as much an extraordinary compilation of quotations as a narrative work in itself), are also well worn. I make no claims to consistency among these works, only that they have resonated with me, as did *Learning from Las Vegas* (1972), by Robert Venturi, Denise Scott Brown, and Steven Izenour, and the writings of J. B. Jackson, collected in *Landscape in Sight: Looking at America* (1997); *A Sense of Place, a Sense of Time*

(1994); and *Discovering the Vernacular Landscape* (1984). I should also mention three distinguished books that helped me to see architecture in new ways: *The Culture of Building* (1999), by Howard Davis, which suggests that architecture takes its form in large part because of inter-relationships among architects, craftsworkers, financiers, contractors, public officials, bankers, planners, and so forth—building "cultures" that have existed in most societies throughout history; *Studies in Tectonic Culture: The Poetics of Construction in Nineteenth and Twentieth Century Architecture* (1995), by Kenneth Frampton, in which an eminent scholar known for his interest in theory analyzes modern architecture in terms of the reality of built form, not abstract ideas; and *The American City: What Works, What Doesn't,* by Alexander Garvin, 2nd ed. (2002), an exceptionally clearheaded analysis of urban planning and urban design that considers aesthetics, politics, finances, history, and culture in equal measure.

For general historical reference, it is still difficult to beat *An Outline of European Architecture,* 7th ed. (1963), by Sir Nikolaus Pevsner, though it stops in the mid-twentieth century; and two volumes in the Pelican History of Art series, *The Architecture of Britain,* by John Summerson, and *Architecture: Nineteenth and Twentieth Centuries,* 4th ed. (1977), by Henry-Russell Hitchcock. Pevsner's *Pioneers of Modern Design, from William Morris to Walter Gropius,* rev. ed. (1964), is an impeccable, if narrowly focused, history of the origins of European modernism; Reyner Banham's *Theory and Design in the First Machine Age* (1967) is somewhat broader in its viewpoint. William H. Jordy and William H. Pierson Jr.'s four-volume *American Buildings and Their Architects* (1970–86) is a superb comprehensive history, as is Leland Roth's one-volume *American Architecture: A History* (2001). G. E. Kidder Smith's *Source Book of American Architecture: 500 Notable Buildings from the 10th Century to the Present* (1996) is an excellent compendium of buildings in the United States, organized in the manner of an encyclopedia; more recently, Jonathan Glancey has done the same thing for a time rather than a place in his *20th C Architecture: The Structures That Shaped the Century* (1998), international in its scope. For the full historical sweep from Stonehenge, the Pyramids, and the pueblos onward, Marvin Trachtenberg and Isabelle Hyman's *Architecture: From Prehistory to Post-Modernism,* 2nd ed. (2002), and Spiro Kostof's *A History of Architecture: Settings and Rituals,* 2nd ed. (1995), are excellent. So is David Watkin's *A History of Western Architecture,* 4th ed. (2005), which is vastly more sympathetic to historical revival and more critical of orthodox modernism than Pevsner's *Outline,* which it roughly resembles in scope, though Watkin carries the story somewhat closer to our time.

This book was written to complement, not to duplicate, such basic reference works. Other references that may be useful are architectural dictionaries, of which *The Penguin Dictionary of Architecture,* 5th ed. (1999), by John Fleming, Hugh Honour, and Nikolaus Pevsner, remains the finest. Cyril M. Harris's *Historic Architecture Sourcebook* (1977) and his *Dictionary of Architecture and Construction,* 4th ed. (2006), are more wide-ranging, and excellent. There are numerous guides to architectural styles; one of my favorites is *How to Read Buildings: A Crash Course in Architectural Styles* (2008), by Carol Davidson Cragoe, in part because it also functions as a more general architectural dictionary. For structure and other aspects of the more technical side of architecture, which my book does not consider in much detail: Edward Allen's *How Buildings Work: The Natural Order of Architecture,* 3rd ed. (2005), and Mario Salvadori's *Why Buildings Stand Up: The Strength of Architecture* (1980). Another category that may not seem directly relevant to this book but which remains essential to me consists of books that I consult regularly about the architecture of New York, many of which have, in fact, turned out to be sources for material in this book: Rem Koolhaas's *Delirious New York: A Retroactive Manifesto for New York,* new ed. (1994); James Sanders's *Celluloid Skyline: New York and the Movies* (2001); Nathan Silver's *Lost New York* (1967); and the extraordinary compendium of works overseen by Robert A. M. Stern and written by Stern in association with David Fishman, Gregory Gilmartin, John Massengale, Thomas Mellins, and Jacob Tilove: *New York 1880, New York 1900, New York 1930, New York 1960,* and *New York 2000* (1999–2006), all of which I feel I could wallow in for days on end.

In the category of more personal books that aspire, as this one does, to help the reader see: James F. O'Gorman's *ABC of Architecture* (1998), which is exceptionally sharp and clear-headed, if quite basic; Stanley Abercrombie's *Architecture as Art* (1986), a more extended lesson and rumination on aesthetics; and Witold Rybczynski's *The Look of Architecture* (2001), an engaging and erudite conversation on the appeal of architecture in general. Philip M. Isaacson's *Round Buildings, Square Buildings, and Buildings That Wiggle Like a Fish* (1988), though technically an introduction to architecture for children, is so gracefully written and intelligently conceived that it can do quite well as a basic book for anyone. Cesar Pelli's *Observations for Young Architects* (1999) is neither as well titled nor as entertainingly written, but it is solid and wise as an introduction. Not strictly an architecture book, but a series of commentaries on design in general, is *Seventy-Nine Short Essays on Design* (2007), a brilliant and witty compendium by the graphic designer Michael Bierut. I am somewhat less enthusiastic about two older books, George Nelson's *How to See: Visual Adventures in a World God Never Made* (1977), in which the great designer tells us quite bluntly what is good and what is not; and *Architecture and You: How to Experience and Enjoy Buildings* (1978), by William Wayne Caudill, William Merriweather Peña, and Paul Kennon, whose architect-authors never break away from jargon as much as they seem to think they have. As writing architects go, Charles Moore and Donlyn Lyndon were far more imaginative and engaging in *Chambers for a Memory Palace* (1994), a book in the form of letters to each other ruminating on different works of architecture; Moore here did what he did best, which was convince you to share his love of the quirky. Not long ago, the philosopher Alain de Botton, in *The Architecture of Happiness* (2006), investigated with eloquence and common sense the question of beauty in architecture and its effect on our sense of contentment. His gentle book is a welcome addition to the list of personal books on looking at architecture that, in our time at least, begins with Steen Eiler Rasmussen's *Experiencing Architecture* (1959), first published a half century ago, and which, if not the liveliest book in the world, is still appealing for its breadth, reason, and clarity.

acknowledgments

This book had its origins a very long time ago, when Jason Epstein, then the editor-in-chief of Random House, suggested to me that there was a need for a book about architecture that would be the equivalent of Aaron Copland's *What to Listen for in Music,* that remarkable volume that is neither a history of music nor an introduction to musical theory but an attempt to explain the nature of musical experience. Copland wrote with the assumption that his readers were interested in music but had no professional knowledge of it; his goal was not to make them professionals but to heighten the connection they felt to an art they were drawn to without always understanding why.

I was excited by the challenge Jason Epstein set before me, and I began work on it. Other books intervened before I could complete this one, and I am especially grateful to John Donatich of Yale University Press for suggesting that I pick up this project after a long interval and complete it for Yale as *Why Architecture Matters.* But I am happy to remember that it is Jason who suggested this book, gave it its initial shape, and edited its first chapters in their early form.

Once the book came to Yale, Ileene Smith has been the writer's dream of the perfect editor. Her commitment to the original idea and her vision in seeing how it could be adapted to become part of a Yale

University Press series have been critical, and she has been a joy to work with. Other thanks are due to Laura Jones Dooley, manuscript editor at the Press, and to Alex Larson at the Press. Erica Stoller, keeper of the great ESTO architectural photo archive, has graciously made so many images available for this book, and I am grateful also to the incomparable Julius Shulman, who took the classic photograph that is the icon of California modernism. None of the photographs here would have been assembled without the invaluable aid of Natalie Matutschovsky, picture researcher extraordinaire, who possesses the perfect balance of efficiency and a keen eye. Under time pressure, she worked with grace. My agent, Amanda Urban, has lived with this project from its origins, and I am grateful to her for easing the transition into its final form.

The purpose of this book, as I say in the Introduction, is "to come to grips with how things"—which is to say works of architecture—"feel to us when we stand before them, with how architecture affects us emotionally as well as intellectually. . . . Its most important message, I hope, is to encourage you to look, and . . . to trust your eye." In many ways my greatest debt is to those who helped me to look, and to trust my own eye, and it is hard to know where to begin or where to end a list of those who I should be thanking here, since it would have to include every architect whose work I have admired, or disliked, or given more than a passing glance to. The buildings mentioned in this book are but a fraction of a lifetime spent looking at buildings, reading about them, thinking about them, and talking about them. One of the pleasures of a life as an architecture critic is that almost every place you go is grist for the mill. But I can single out a number of people who have played a larger role in shaping my visual sensibility, either through their work or through conversations about architecture that we have had over the years, among them Kent Barwick, Laurie Beckleman, Robert Bookman, Richard Brettell, Denise Scott Brown, Adele Chatfield-Taylor, David Childs, Jack Davis, David Dunlap, David Freeman, Alexander Garvin, Frank Gehry, Allan Greenberg, Charles Gwathmey, Christopher Hawthorne, Patrick Hickox, Ada Louise Huxtable, Philip Johnson, Richard Kahan,

Charles Kaiser, Blair Kamin, Kent Kleinman, Eden Ross Lipson, Michael Lykoudis, Richard Meier, Charles Moore, Nicolai Ouroussoff, Renzo Piano, Steven Rattner, Steven Robinson, Clifford Ross, David Schwarz, Paul Segal, Michael Sorkin, Robert A. M. Stern, Stanley Tigerman, Robert Venturi, Steven Weisman, and Leonard Zax.

I owe deep thanks also to David Remnick, the editor of the *New Yorker,* who for the past decade has given me the chance to continue to sharpen my critical eye on all aspects of the built environment for the magazine. There is no greater place in journalism to have as one's home. I have been privileged to have taught for the past few years at Parsons The New School for Design in New York City, where I served as dean before I had the good sense to move into the classroom and where my colleagues in the Master of Architecture thesis studio, Stella Betts, Eric Bunge, Reid Freeman, David Leven, Astrid Lipka, Mark Rakatansky, Henry Smith-Miller, and Peter Wheelwright—along with our students —have made me understand more than ever the complexity and the delicacy of the process by which architectural ideas take form.

But at the top of the list of influences, academic and otherwise, I would have to put Vincent Scully. To me he has been far more than a professor of architectural history: he taught me not only about architecture but about the essential relationship of architecture to all of culture, and about the profound connection that architecture can have to both the written and the spoken word. He has been a treasured friend for more than four decades, going back to the time that he inspired me as a student to channel my love of architecture into a life's work and helped me to understand that there is little point to a life that is not spent following your passions.

I once ended the acknowledgments of a book by thanking my wife, Susan, and my son Adam for "the most precious gift: impatience." This book has had too long a gestation period for impatience to be of much use, but I do know that my family has once again been there, supporting my work and the idea of returning to this project, the origins of which stretch back to a time when two of my three sons, now grown, were small children. Susan knew that I would not be satisfied until I picked this book up again and finished it. She has, as always, been an insightful and essential reader all along the way. She and my three sons, Adam, Ben, and Alex, give me what a family should: love, and more than few gentle nudges. They are my most valued critics and my most beloved friends.

illustration credits

University, 62; Peter Mauss/Esto, 203; Norman McGrath, courtesy Hugh Hardy, 206; Municipal Art Society of New York Archives, 207; National Gallery of Art, Washington, D.C., Gallery Archives, 131; Cervin Robinson/Library of Congress, 198; Paul Rudolph Foundation, 133; Ole Scheeren/Office for Metropolitan Architecture (OMA), 95; Pepo Segura/Fundació Mies van der Rohe, Barcelona, 11; Walter Smalling, Jr./Library of Congress, 119; Lee Stalsworth, 88; Ezra Stoller/Esto, 77, 80, 115, 116, 121; David Sundberg/Esto, 176, 200; Jack Woods/Warner Bros. Pictures/Photofest, 161; Steve Zucker, 105

index

Page numbers in *italics* refer to illustrations

Stern, Robert A. M., 58, 190; 15 Central Park West, 215, 216
Stone, Edward Durell, 75, 78; General Motors Building, 75–80, *80*, 81–82, 87
style, xiv, 34, 70, 74, 75, 154; as language, 189; reused from the past, 34; time and, 34, 182–94. *See also specific architectural styles*
suburbs, x–xi, 3, 142, 144, 146, 225–26; edge cities, 228–32; personal memories of, 146–48; sprawl, 231
Sullivan, Louis, xii, 100, 106; facades of, 100; Owatonna Bank, 107
Summerson, Sir John, 181, 197, 199; *Heavenly Mansions,* 197; *The Unromantic Castle,* 171
supermarkets, 147–48
Sydney Opera House, 8, 16

Taj Mahal, xii, 72, 125
Tate Modern, London, 195
technology, xiii, 193–94, 224–28; cyberspace, 224–28, 229; time and, 193–94
television, 155, 162, 228
tenements, 5–6
texture, xiv, 99, 127, 128, 137, 154, 218
30 St. Mary Axe tower, London, 92, 93
Tiffany and Company, New York, 191
time and buildings, 171–211, 226; change and, 173–74; modernist architecture and, 177–94, 208; place and, 192–93; preservation of older architecture, 195–211; repu-

tation and, 181–82; skyscrapers and, 174–77, 185–86, 191, 193–94; style and, 34, 183–94; technology and, 193–94; World Trade Center, 174–77; Yale Art and Architecture Building, 178–82
Time-Life Building, New York, 150
Times Square, New York, 142, 150
Townhouse, 18 West Eleventh Street, New York, 205–6, *206*
townhouses, 205–6, 217–19
train stations, 117–18, 150, 185, 197–98, 199–200, 207–9
Trinity Church, Boston, 79
Trinity Church, New York, 151
Turnbull, William, 97
Turner, J. M. W., 156
TWA Terminal, Kennedy Airport, New York, 75, 116–17, 120, 121, 194; interior view, 116, *116*, 117

Unitarian Church, Rochester, New York, 44, *45*, 134
Unité d'Habitation, Marseilles, 75
United Nations, New York, 25, 97
Unity Temple, Oak Park, Illinois, 47, 112, 134, 136, 138
University of Virginia, Charlottesville, 12–15, 42, 43, 107; Lawn, 13–14, *14*
urban design and architecture, 214–32; cyberspace and, 224–28, 229; edge cities, 228–32; New Urbanism, 231–32; similarity in, 214–15, 217–19, 221, 225–26; streets, 214–24

152–55, 185; Art and Architecture
Building (Paul Rudolph Hall),
132–33, *133,* 152, 178–79, *179,* 180–
82; Harkness Tower, 60–61, *62,*
185, 186; Ingalls Rink, 120–21, *121,*
152, 194; Jeffrey Loria Hall, *179;*
Memorial Quadrangle, 60, 185

Yamasaki, Minoru, 175; Rainer
Square skyscraper, 57–58, 60;
World Trade Center, 174–75, *176,*
177